New Life in Catholic Schools

By the Same Author

Blueprint for a Catholic University

Christian Ethics

New Life in Catholic Schools

BY

LEO R. WARD

Congregation of Holy Cross

B. HERDER BOOK CO.

15 & 17 South Broadway, St. Louis 2, Mo.

AND *33 Queen Square, London, W.C.*

Library of Congress Catalog Card Number: 58-10551

NIHIL OBSTAT
        William F. Cunningham, C.S.C.
        Censor deputatus

IMPRIMI POTEST
        Theodore J. Mehling, C.S.C.
        Provincial Superior

IMPRIMATUR
        ✠ Leo A. Pursley, D.D.
        Bishop of Fort Wayne

March 20, 1958

Printed in the United States of America by the
Vail-Ballou Press, Inc., Binghamton, New York

»×«

Contents

New Life in Catholic Schools

New Lease on Life

LIKE other social institutions, the school needs new inspiration, new life, an occasional shot in the arm. The school and learning sometimes get this pickup and get it in a big way. But this has happened so seldom that just a few great moments stand out like peaks in the history of Western learning.

Athens in its heyday, aristocratic, pagan and all, was one of those peaks, and has ever since remained the envy and beacon of great men and great societies. The time of Alcuin and Charlemagne, though comparatively something less than a peak, did give a new and great lift of permanent value to learning just when learning had in many senses fallen down nearly to the foot of the hill. The twelfth and thirteenth centuries did it again, at first by combining logical and theological studies and then blossoming out into many fields including professional ones, and with such abandon and freedom as to give mankind the "university" in much its present form. The Renaissance, too, was among other things a kind of new madness for learning, a rebirth of vital interest in ancient civilizations and above all in their learnings, and as lately as twenty years ago the Irish Jesuit, Timothy Corcoran, contributing to Eyre's *European Civilization*, said that the Renaissance as a rebirth of learning is still felt in all the lecture halls of Europe. Modern science is evidently our new learning, and with its zest for knowing nature —beyond other knowers, scientists are finding joy in learning—and with its method and its seemingly inexhaustible fecundity in discovery, it keeps pouring in new materials or content for learning: soft materials at the top, someone has said; and it demands and is likely to supply a new form of learning.

American Catholic schools and indeed all Occidental schools are heirs in many ways to those great visions and achievements, and in the line of intrepidation, to put things at a minimum, these Catholic schools may claim some achievements of their own. This book is written in the conviction that a new Catholic vision is conceivable and is demanded. At least we need a revision and a reliving of some old vital Catholic vision. We will not settle for less.

In order that our schools be great schools what must be the central, driving motive of them? What must they see as their proper good and end? What are the great positive values now accessible in and through

American Catholic education? What should be their value of values and their end of ends? Given American freedoms and opportunities and given the drive shown in Catholic schools for well over a century, what are those schools to do now? How are they to catch a vision and to realize it?

These are the types of questions which we must ask and keep asking. But even in these first lines we say that we shall emphasize the positive, looking mainly to the great good to be done. Only a blinded man could fail to see that Catholic education in America has already done heroic things—with how little equipment and at how big a cost! So far, so good. But what must it do now to be worthy of its opportunities, of its evident dynamism, and of our political, religious, and academic freedom?

These are questions we ask and try to answer in this book, and we think the questions and any serious attempt to answer them must be of interest and really of concern to all educational leaders, whatever their religions and philosophies, and also to many leaders in church and society. It must be a limp sort of citizen who would be apathetic toward or hostile toward so big a segment of American schools: the nuns teaching in American schools certainly exceed 90,000, and we have only ten times that number in all other schools. They must be well prepared for teaching one in ten of our future citizens, and all of us must be actively concerned to help them to be well prepared.

It is fortunate for education in America that a basic problem along the line of our own bothersome questions has been raised. In 1955, Monsignor John Tracy Ellis, professor of church history at the Catholic University in Washington, asked the simple and yet disturbing question, "Do American Catholic schools produce scholars?" Everyone knows the answer: Of course they do—all schools produce scholars. Yes, and no; Catholic schools succeed and fail, and if in regard to scholarship they are like American schools in general, still they fail and have always failed to reach this noble end. They fail to turn out their share of research men of top quality and scholars of top quality; the figures have often proved this truth. A more serious thing, it seems to us, is the fact that they fail to produce a deep and abiding interest in learning and respect for it. To take one notable group: what percentage of American priests believes in scholarship, science, and research as Pope Pius XII believes in them?

The Ellis reply was not exactly a novel one. It had been given before, by men such as Dr. Herzfeld, Sir Hugh Stott Taylor, and the late John M. Cooper. But their replies were limited to particular fields and were based on current material. Dr. Ellis's reply is the first one well grounded historically and aiming to give a comprehensive coverage.

Yet the results of the Ellis publication have been extremely encouraging, and we believe the same may

be said for the results of the article by the Jesuit,
Gustave Weigel.[1] One good result is that people have
not tried to hide the question or the answer, or to explain the whole problem away. No apologist or casuist
of any consequence has appeared.

The reply, and the results, too, have unfortunately
left us pretty much where we were. "Where do we
go from here?" That is the big question, a question
outside Dr. Ellis's and Dr. Weigel's inquiry. Naturally that question was left standing naked.

The immediate good results, however, are obvious,
and are these two. First, the authors' sharp uncom-
promising procedure found a warm reception, and
not primarily among defeatists and cynics, but among
people who believe in man and God. People wanted
to know the actual situation. Second, the background
reasons assigned, especially by Dr. Ellis, have made
many people begin to think about what we are to do.
Among others, several bishops have spoken to the
point.

The negative side is fairly strong in this matter,
and, unhappily, many people seem to thrive on the
negative. They get more worked up over the Communist threat to Christian democratic values than

[1] John Tracy Ellis, "American Catholics and the Intellectual
Life," an article in *Thought*, XXX (Autumn 1955), pp. 351–388;
published in book form under the same title (Chicago: The
Heritage Foundation Inc., 1956). Gustave Weigel, "American
Catholic Intellectualism—a Theologian's Reflections," *Review
of Politics*, XIX (July 1957), pp. 275–308.

over devotion to the values themselves. Down with Communism! But up with what? Name the good which we pursue with such love and vigor that we would gladly die for it. "Do we produce scholars?" That is a troublesome question. How do we propose to produce them and to produce a deep abiding interest in learning—this may be a much more difficult question.

Reacting to the situation, this book dares to face some inevitable tasks. With a too brief reference to the past and continuing creative developments in American Catholic education—the record is manifest to everyone except a Blanshard—we shall attempt to put as clearly and forcibly as possible the matter of a Christian philosophy and a general Christian learning. Roughly, this problem is as follows: In this or that field and again in all fields, do Christians know exactly as pagans know, and do they know simply what pagans know? Do they know differently at all, and do they know different things at all? That is the question. It is a fundamental one, and precisely on the reply to it we are going to keep asking the American Catholic school system, good and recklessly sacrificial as it is, to surpass itself.

In the Catholic school we may not let other good ends, such as piety or propaganda or missionary efforts, stand in the way of Catholic learning. That is in part our position. But then why may we not? Because the Catholic school has a proper good work to do. Of course, Catholic education must in theory and practice keep track of the relation of Christian theology to all other learnings, a matter that is relatively routine and taken for granted.

Besides, we want to raise two new and rather closely related questions, which in any case are being raised by events. One is that of Catholic Action as possibly a form of learning, and Catholic Action, by the way, ties in well with the American practical temper and with what the American Catholic school on the lower levels is now doing best. The other question is that of study and teaching and learning as an apostolate, study and teaching and learning in history, arithmetic, and world religions as well as in Catholic dogma.

We do not by any means write this book to raise these questions, but we shall insist on raising them. They are raised by the times and they stand knocking at the door of any educational philosophy. But we shall undertake to show that these practical issues cannot profitably be raised, and much less profitably answered, until the two prior and much more basic problems of Christian learning and a theoretic Christian and non-Christian learning are raised and adjudicated.

Let us put the difficulty about Christian learning into hypothetical form. If a Christian learning is possible or perhaps even actual, all of us in colleges, whether secular or church-related, would like to know the fact; and since we believe so much in freedom of learning we would like to study the fact in all its implications. If no such learning is possible, we should find that out, too—and say it. If, as Cardinal Stritch says, theology should permeate schools from kindergarten through university, we should realize that truth, also, and build curricula and relevant practices on it. What a job that would be!

The "Christian learning" part of our effort is bound to be slightly technical, but it is the decisive part. Another main part is really a distinct part of the whole which is Christian learning, and is the practical part since, so we shall argue, Catholic Action techniques today offer people in school and out of it a method of acquiring Christian practical wisdom. We shall argue that "CA" should now be given its full and proper chance to do its concentrated share in the whole business of learning, above all in learning how to build Christian communities.

Of course, doing anything practical such as running a school is controlled by the thing's ends, and ends may be either clearly or vaguely seen. What do we run Catholic schools for and what should we run them for? The questions seem simple enough.

We might evade the issue and say that we run schools for a lot of ends—the good of the child, and the nation, and the Church, and peace, and the honor of God, and even for learning. Yet the question remains: What is the major, dominating, overwhelming end and aim of Catholic schools? Catholics build and maintain these schools at an immense cost, as organized Labor in California has remarked. Now, what would be lost to America and mankind if Catholic schools did not exist? The questions may not be dodged: What in fact is their dominating aim, and what ideally should be their dominating aim?

Our Catholic schools were set up to save the faith and morals of boys and girls. That is an historical fact about which there is not the slightest doubt. That was and that remains their major, dominating end. That is what they were set up for and that is what they still operate for. They were not set up to produce learning at all, let alone scholarship or an abiding interest in learning; and it was incidental that they assumed and that they have progressively assumed an interest in learning and scholarship. At the start they were more like missions than like schools, and to this day many a Catholic school is a cross between a mission, a parish, and a school, and a fairly well "integrated" cross, at that. Here we have an obvious and important reason why Catholic schools have not in general produced learning and scholarship—they were not established to produce them. In this book, we waive the question whether they have done well the work they were set up to do and whether they continue to do it well.

Dr. Ellis and others give us good reasons why scholarship and scholars have been fairly well outside the products of those schools. For instance, Dr. Ellis says that Catholics in this country were poor, were harshly dealt with, driven into a ghetto, discriminated against; most Catholics came—even the Irish and Germans, not to mention the Poles and Italians—as relatively late immigrants; and they have borne and continue to bear a double tax load, supporting schools they patronize and those they don't patronize. These reasons are well authenticated and tell much of the story of why Catholic schools lag in interest in learning and scholarship.

They are not the most important reason. The most important reason, insufficiently emphasized by Dr. Ellis, is that they were not set up for scholarship or primarily for learning at all, and even now only some few of them begin to operate briskly to produce a high interest in learning and of course even fewer of them operate to produce top-flight scholars. Here is the most important reason for the condition which so many deplore. An institution not set up or operated to produce scholars and a high interest in learning is not likely to produce them. It might do so, but the chances are against such a result. We will do well to produce scholars and interest in learning if we set out to produce them.

To achieve such great social ends requires devotion and hard work. That goes without saying. But from first to last it also requires a certain purity of aim. Blessed are the pure of heart, for they shall see

God. They shall see God because there is little between them and God, little distracting self-love, earth-
love, and profit-love. Something the same holds for
those who go for learning. They need to be so pure
of heart that they will not let things get in their
way. And not only things, but they will not let even
great high motives distract them. The pure of heart
go for learning and they will see it and reach it.

The point may be put in another way. Take the
thousands of nuns sacrificing their lives in American
schools. What has been their aim in this work? Has
it in general really been to help children to understand God and nature and man? The nun is high-
idealled and high-motivated. She teaches in order to
sanctify her own soul and to save "little souls." Priests
have been and still are building new schools and running schools with never a first thought and hardly a
compelling thought at all for anyone's understanding
anything, but with first and compelling thoughts for
saving the faith and morals of children.

We don't scold them for having these wonderful
and incomparable ends and motives. These ends are
exactly what American Catholic schools were set up
for in the first place. All documents clearly show this.
In his first pastoral letter (1792) Archbishop Carroll,
our first American-born bishop, urged the need of
"a pious and Catholic education of the young to in-
sure their growing up in the faith." The urgency of
the situation is repeated over and over from that time,

and the way to meet the situation is repeated as often; for example, by the First Provincial Council of Baltimore (1829) and by the First and Second and Third Plenary Council of Baltimore (1852, 1868, and 1884).[1]

The piety motive and the faith motive are incontestably there and incontestably high; they are still there and will remain. It is another question whether these motives have at times distracted teachers and students and perhaps left school people less pure of heart to do their school work than we might wish. It is like school children getting so tangled up with play that they lose interest in study. Let us then summarize again the reasons urged by Dr. Ellis for the unsatisfactory result, and emphasize what we think by far the biggest single reason: Catholics in America were too busy, said Dr. Ellis, too poor, too despised, too materialistic—and, we add, too distracted by better things—to love knowledge and pursue it with joy and abandon.

Other reasons why Catholic schools have lagged in producing the liveliest zeal for learning and scholarship are valid and important. But the "save the faith and morals" reason is valid, and is decisive. In order to do something about the situation, people must begin to see that a chief reason for the shortcoming is this unlikely one. The highest "save the soul" motives

[1] See Leo R. Ward, *Blueprint for a Catholic University* (St. Louis: B. Herder Book Co., 1949), pp. 284–289.

tend to get in the way of simple, plebeian intellectual ends. Shall we say they "tend at times" to this effect? No, we say they tend to it. Now it is ironic that the best should sometimes defeat the good. But a weed is a plant out of place, and it is a "weed" because its presence there is hurting the growth of other plants. We think that may at times be the way with heavenly motives and ideals in schools. How good they are, and yet sometimes how like a weed!

These incomparable motives and ideals may hurt in two ways. The child, especially in the grades, has often been kept swathed and bathed in piety, so that, floating in piety, it has been hard for him to get down to the business in hand, which may be as humdrum as reading and arithmetic or the first steps in science. He has learnt to revere angels and saints, and good for him that he has, but perhaps both his teacher and himself have sometimes failed to put a razor-keen edge on respect and reverence for elementary mathematics and elementary science. (People won't believe that in one parochial school—just one—the eighth-graders sing the seven canonical hours five days a week.) The second way they could hurt is this. Teachers with ideals out of this world may at times have let piety, not to say dogma, substitute for knowledge and the hard, everyday work required for getting knowledge. Some teachers now and then may have been confused and let such a substitution rule the roost in their own case, and in the student's case.

Two famous Frenchmen have said what we are just now saying and have explained how tricks of piety can hurt knowledge. The well-known Christian philosopher, Professor Gilson, has put the whole thing in these positive and plain words: *"Piety never dispenses with technique.* For technique is that without which even the most lively piety is incapable of using nature for God."* Gilson's idea is that to learn arithmetic or geography we have to learn it, and learning an art or a science requires habits of discipline and work. The well-known novelist, François Mauriac, has also summed up the danger of piety precluding study: "I lay it down as a fact that not a student of my class was able to answer, even in a rough way, the sort of objection that a Catholic should have had an answer to in those first years of the century. As if to even matters up, our teachers excelled in enveloping us with a heavenly atmosphere that bathed every instant of the day: they formed not Catholic minds, but Catholic feelings." [1]

Nuns are the typical teachers in Catholic schools, and possibly they sometimes lack purity of heart in forming intelligences, in helping children to come to love and respect knowledge. Brother-teachers and priest-teachers stand in the same peril, and perhaps priests above all, because of their authority in schools and society. How big a percentage of these school

[1] From *God and Mammon*, by François Mauriac, published by Sheed and Ward, Inc., New York, p. 36.

teachers and school superintendents really believe in knowledge and are keen for at least some art or science? Some of them, a joy to meet, really do want to bring out minds. But it is asking a good deal to expect them in general to give first place at school to any such belief and love.

We need many things in American schools, the Catholic schools included; e.g., we need teachers, buildings, and funds; but what we need most is a freer look at intellectual ends, so that we may adopt a freer and more dynamic-creative aim for all schools, simply as schools.

This bold book will try to state such an end for Catholic schools, an end which the author thinks a dynamic-creative end, itself properly and directly an intellectual end, and at the same time properly and directly a Christian intellectual end entirely in line with the best things Christian schools have ever done. At present, we merely assert our position and shall later try to justify it. We assert that *the* end of our schools is Christian intellectual life. We assert that in schools the main business is not to convert people, to make them good or to save their faith and morals— good ends all of them. In some circumstances, an inherently lower act or aim must rate highest; for instance, it is better to give a starving man some soup than to pray for him: and good as it is to pray for him, we should not let the praying get in the way of the soup. All through this book we say that the tremendous high end of Christian schools, an end considerably lower than the end of life and the universe, is Christian intellectual life.

Two things at the outset about "Christian intellectual life." It must be intellectual life, and it must be Christian. The one thing that we Christian teachers and directors of schools must learn is to be pure of heart in relation to that aim. This life and learning— and don't pretend that we already have it in abundance —requires a difficult *re*-learning, a conversion and re-orientation. We ought to have schools merely to introduce us to this re-orientation itself, since it is not now regularly learned in seminaries or novitiates or Catholic teachers' colleges. The unlearning and *re*-learning will cost much; we will suffer growing pains. A people is not converted in a day—a people with high, confused motives and ideals.

We believe that dynamic-creative ends are available. They could be stated and could be pursued. The main problem is to become free enough to see them and to pursue them. Fortunately, the ends are now to some extent pursued. But like displaced persons, they often have to take their chances in the underground.

To aid in beginning to make our chief point clear, we repeat: strange indeed if such lofty ideals and motives, the saving of faith and morals and apology for the faith, should turn out to be a primary factor in preventing Catholic schools, so nobly founded and maintained, from doing their properest and fullest work for persons and the total community of America and the world.

The problem posed by their relative failure as schools, a matter made much of by Dr. Ellis, Dr. Weigel, Father John Cavanaugh and others, is something to ponder. But our emphasis throughout is going to be on the positive. For we think it possible to state not only what has been their greatest initial and continuing handicap, but what must be the remedy. We have said that the handicap in question has been a sort of magnificent, high-idealled confusion, and we are raising quite a distinctive issue, namely, whether it is not possible to be dominated by high and mighty ideals and yet to avoid confusion. If it is available, we want an unconfused basic ideal, solid as a rock, proper to schools and at the same time creative and dynamic. Such an ideal end is available. Certainly it is needed, and it is deserved by the whole American Catholic educational establishment.

Next we come to a prestatement of a secondary point of the book. The second confusion is a perversion that affects all American schools, and most of all the colleges and universities. What is in fact the dominating end for which American colleges and universities train students? Undoubtedly the dominating end in some of our small church-related colleges is a religious one. But for the most part the thing the big colleges and universities do is to advance the economic interests of individuals. That is their effective end;

that is what they do. It is the old individualistic, self-seeking end, an end which by the way dominates more than the college and the college man. The college says in effect: "I came that you should seek your own self and do it more efficiently." The college abets an aim which on the contrary it should be finding ways to transcend. The college and university now fall in line so naturally with the ways of business that their administrators often use business jargon rather than academic jargon: they know it better and are more at home with it. They seem to be trapped by the "organizational compulsions" of modern technical and industrial society.[1]

This is no doubt to be expected. Still, the problem of the final cause or end of the whole educational process has again and again to be considered. Do we in colleges simply help people to help themselves? And if so, do we really need to do this, and is it our proper function to do it? Now, to say the least, the self-seeking drive is deep in man, and with St. Thomas Aquinas we think that it is present and operative in all being. In any case, we know that people are vigorously self-seeking, and a major task of education in and out of school is to help people learn to live beyond themselves and serve the good of community. Our

[1] William H. Whyte's *Organization Man* (New York: Simon and Shuster, 1956) seems justified in classing the college or university administrator as another instance of the "organization man."

total schooling has to teach young persons to be looking for ways and actually finding ways of perpetually
transcending self-love and self-seeking. Habits must
be formed of transcending and transmuting self for
the good of man. So much the worse for us if Communism has had to recall us to this truth.

Learning how to transcend self, learning how to
love and serve the community—these are learnings of
some kind. What techniques do we have in Catholic
or other schools to afford encouragement to and a
chance to acquire these learnings? Since self-seeking
is strong in human beings and the human race, we are
sure to find it everywhere. But it is especially strong
in the modern Occident, having been sanctioned by
private interpretation and *laissez faire;* and it may be
that the self-seeking drive is stronger in America even
than in Europe, though for any who have lived in
Europe the possibility is not easy to imagine.

For the sake of argument let us say that the self-
seeking drive is not always present in every action;
that it is not stronger in the Occident than in the
Orient, nor stronger in America than in Europe. Still,
in and out of school, men have to learn how to form
a community, learn to live for others, to give much
of their lives for them; and this book is going to advance the proposition that Catholic Action is an admirable technique for this "learning how."

Right or wrong, then, our claims amount to a head-
on attack on problems, and we are happy to throw in

our weight toward solving problems of what we have just called confusion and perversion. What do our schools produce, what don't they produce, what should they produce—these are major questions because they are questions about ends, and, as Aristotle and Aquinas remark, in the order of things to be done, ends are the most important causes. If men are wrong on the ends of schools, they are as wrong as men can be: at each moment they have the wrong principle on tap. All our rightness about the ends of the universe cannot then save us from this wrongness in a particular field and work. We are simply wrong—that's all. Then ironically enough, we are shocked to find that in this field things don't come out right. Of course they don't. We are like a truck driver who is right on the ends of the universe, but wrong about how to drive a truck and the purposes of driving trucks. Right as he is, he is all mixed up, and he is going to get freakish and unhappy results.

Loaded down with super-ideals, our schools may turn out to be like the truck driver. At least, Dr. Ellis and others often repeat that in the one thing necessary the schools are falling below par. We say and will go on saying that the great ends they mainly seek—the saving of the faith, the direct glory of God, and the aggrandizement of individuals—are not the proper specific ends of schools and learning. Twenty years ago a man zealous for the good of Catholic schools said well indeed part of what we want to say. The

Catholic educator's enemies, that Jesuit said,[1] are often those of his own household: "They call upon the ultimate objective of all Catholic life, the glory of God and the salvation of souls, and attempt to make this do duty as the immediate and specific object of education. They have forgotten that the end of education, as such, is specific and distinct from the end of missionary activity; that to confound the ultimate end of both with the formal and immediate object of each, is to introduce disorder into the whole Catholic scheme."

Let us take the statement of that vigorous man at its word, and see which principles are necessary if we are to introduce a fundamental order into the "Catholic scheme" of education. For the sake of argument at least, let us take Dr. Ellis and Dr. Weigel at their word, too, and see what must be done now so as to begin to bring the American Catholic school, which represents such marvelous Christian and American leadership, up to its native potentialities.

[1] George Bull, S.J., *America*, April 23, 1938, p. 55.

A Christian Learning

IN THE face of knowledge and intellectual development, Christians have passed through several stages,
each of them readily intelligible in its setting. Briefly
and roughly stated, here they are.

First. Little conscious about problems of knowing,
the first Christians, with St. Paul as a vivid exemplar,
were busy converting Jews and Greeks and Romans
and building Christian communities. Some apostles
were fishermen, but all were men who could preach
and write in a foreign language, and St. John and
St. Paul were learned men. The apostles were not
opening schools in the ordinary sense of this term, and
were not engaged in the study of Grecian philosophy
or Roman poetry.

Second. What need have we of secular learning?
What communication can there be between light and
darkness, between Paul and Apollo? That is the way

Tertullian (d.230) put the matter in his *Apologeticus*. He thought he had thus closed the question, and many others have thought the question—perhaps all questions—closed. Some still think so. An old priest-teacher once came to me with a popular little book in his hands. "See here," he shouted, "what this fellow says: 'Young people go to college to get a philosophy!' Good God, man, we've got a philosophy!"

Third. Despite the neatness and simplicity of the reply, and despite the exclusiveness with which some would take Christ's words, "Teach what I have commanded you," St. Jerome and St. Augustine took another view which has in general been the Christian view for fifteen centuries. In his letter to Magus (no. 70) St. Jerome asked whether Moses and the prophets did not use materials from writings by Gentiles, and he remarked that St. Paul used pagan inscriptions and pagan poets. In his *De doctrina Christiana* St. Augustine said that to understand the Scriptures we need to lean on secular learnings: Hebrew, Greek, and Latin, and "nature," numbers and music; history also, he said, and physics, rhetoric, and logic are useful to the Christian in search of eternal life. Here was quite a different view, making out a case for the marriage of secular and biblical learning. Augustine said that the highest teaching is in the Bible, but that if the philosophers' teachings harmonize with truth and faith we should turn them to account; in such circumstances, St. Augustine said, pagans are unjust possessors of truths discovered by them, and those truths belong more to us than to them.

Whatever of Augustine's "just" and "unjust," the principle is established—Christians may never go back on learning, on any little or big, secular or spiritual learning; there is to be a marriage of the two; and on the terms of the marriage Augustine himself will have something decisive to say. The result is the Western intellectual tradition, begun by the Greeks and continued to our day by Jews and Christians.

Fourth. Through a long age rough on intellectual life, the Jerome-Augustine ideal managed to survive, until in the twelfth and the thirteenth centuries it had a realization in a new birth of learning. At the start of the ninth century, Alcuin, who was Charlemagne's superintendent of schools, declared (so the tradition goes) for a new Athens, but a Christian one. It was yet some centuries before learning came fully alive and universities came to be ranked as one of the three top institutions in society, along with Church and State. Most distinguished of the popes on learning was Gregory IX, who repeatedly spoke for both the good and the freedom of learning, and in his Magna Carta of university life (1231) as well as in his defense of the students at Cambridge University (1233), he expressed the ideal of the university freely dedicated to wisdom. He said: "Since in the Church of God men of letters shine as a candle on the candlestick [and] through their teaching faithful people are directed in the path of justice, we rightly wish to and we ought to provide that they who are busy with the science of letters . . . should be free to pursue their purpose of study." He was perhaps the first to feature the workshop idea, calling Paris

> mother of sciences,
> city of letters, where
> as in a special workshop of wisdom [1]
> skillful men ornament and decorate
> the precious stones of the spouse of Christ.

For several hundred years, from Rabanus Maurus (d.856) through Thomas Aquinas (d.1274) and through Descartes (d.1650), the problem was not the neglect of reason, but almost the overweening trust in it, to the possible neglect of intuition and of a theory of learning through living, or through what is now called learning by "connaturality" or "congeniality." Through those centuries men wanted to take even the revealed mysteries out of the area of mystery and find rational proof for them. The "pro" and "con" of everything had to be put down in syllogisms, and the title of Abelard's *Sic et Non* ("Yes and No") as well as the title of Peter the Lombard's *Sententiae* ("Opinions") suggests the passion that people had "to be rational" and to say everything that could be said for and against anything that men held. It was the era of Christian rationalism, which of

[1] *In officina sapientiae speciali.*

course continues in various degrees among most Christians. It is well suggested in the formula used eventually by the Cambridge Platonists against the obscurantist fideism of the Puritans. These Christian Platonists said: "Reason is the candle of the Lord, lighted by God and lighting us to God."

Fifth. With the dying down of that intellectual fire and the coming of a new learning called the Renaissance, and above all that called the Reformation, the Christian zeal for learning, which of course had always been checkered, in effect did some back-tracking. It was as if the Christian lost faith in learning. What really happened was that he became busy with other matters. The Reformation meant many things, and it certainly meant a world at religious war for many generations, continuing in some ways to our time and place: and war is not good for learning. The learned Christian, Catholic or Protestant, found himself engaged in controversy, propaganda, and apology. He was less free than he had been to love and pursue arts and sciences, and these were no longer commonly sought as they had been, as simply good, as goods justified in themselves. Arts and sciences had to be subordinated to a work to be done, and were used as a weapon in a world at war. In various degrees, the scholar lacked freedom, and this suffering has affected both the Catholic and the Protestant scholar. To take an extreme example, Paul Blanshard, a man with some knowledge and much native intellectual power, is obviously prejudiced, feeling that he has to attack and destroy Catholics; and thus he is not free to do objective scientific studies. Propagandists and warriors are the poorest and least free students.

Hamstrung in this way for centuries, Christian learning has suffered immeasurable losses. It also became fearful and apologetic for a time, among Catholics and Protestants, in the face of science. People talked about the "conflict," a kind of fomented war, between religion and science. The problem was to see how scriptural and theological teachings meshed with discoveries in science; and a main concern of great churchmen-scholars, e.g., Cardinal Newman, was to show that no real conflict existed. That day of fear and apology is well past,[1] and it is a confused or a dishonest man who claims present actuality for it. But for a long time it had its effect and served to cripple learning.

Sixth. That brings us to the special American problem where learning among Catholics, as Dr. Ellis shows, has suffered from circumstances foreign to its nature; but where, we must add, there is a dynamism and a spirit of sacrifice which—once it begins to be rightly aimed—will accomplish great things.

---

[1] The fear today is on the part of scientists, some of whom stand in trepidation before their own discoveries and what these may do to mankind; but some scientists also want to know how new scientific knowledge relates to ethics and religion. See *Bulletin of Atomic Scientists*, Dec., 1956; also Jan. and March, 1957.

Among Christians learning has suffered in many
ways and thrived in many ways, and the latter are
much more important. Now the chief learnings by
which men live are two; namely, wisdom and prudence; and at least in the Western world, we have
obtained our wisdom mainly from two sources, a
Grecian-pagan source, and a Hebrew-Christian
source; and our prudential knowledge comes above
all from the latter source. But before the chapters
where we pass wisdom and prudence in review as
central types of learning, we want to consider what
we are to understand, if we are to understand anything, by a "Christian learning," a "Christian school,"
and a "Christian scholar." Can these terms make any
living, operative sense in America today? This fundamental question is a difficult one, in itself complicated, and for a long time badly confused. A chief
purpose of this book is to try to disengage the real
and urgent question of "Christian learning," and to
force ourselves to look squarely at the possible answers. This we attempt in the present chapter and its
successor; then we give a special chapter to the notion
of "Christian school."

The wealth in the American Catholic schools is
the army of dedicated people. These people are doing
great work, and yet, according to competent obser-
vers, an immense potential has so far relatively failed
to be actualized. The wish of Pius XII as expressed in
his addresses (1951 and 1952) to women religious is

that this potential come to fulfillment.[1] We think the reasons for the relative waste and failure are mainly two. One reason, as we said, is that these schools are sometimes in part distracted from the primary and direct-line work of schools: we say "sometimes," "in part," but just as strongly we say "distracted." The other reason which we want to take up now is more a confusion than a distraction. It is a lack of clear understanding of the one thing necessary.

If anything is necessary in a Christian school, it is Christian learning. We had better therefore have a clear understanding of that learning, and this under-standing we take to be the fundamental, number-one problem in philosophy of Christian education: that is, if "Christian education" can make any sense at all.

To begin with, we note that the school is an or-ganized social institution, common for a long time now in the Occident,[2] for helping the child to pass relatively out of his primal ignorance into whatever light of day is possible for man. The end in this tradi-tional view is learning: it is post-ignorance. But "learn-ing" is a big, over-all concept with many meanings and implications. In general, it means the same for a Christian as for a pagan. In learning there is a partic-ular union between learner and learnt, between know-

---

[1] See *The Mind of the Church in the Formation of Sisters* (New York: Fordham University Press, 1956).

[2] Cf. H. I. Marrou, *A History of Education in Antiquity*, Tr. by George Lamb (New York: Sheed and Ward, 1956).

ing subject and known object. In assimilating food
there is a merging and a union between bodies; and in
chemical changes, two or more bodies become one.

The union between knower and known is special
and unique. The being and meaning-essence of tree
are, when tree is known by man, left there in the
forest where the tree stood all the time. But the being
and meaning-essence of tree are somehow taken, by
force of knowledge powers—by sight and touch and
intellect—into the knower, and become one being
with him. He "knows" this tree and he knows "tree."
The senses get—"grasp" is the word used in all languages for sensible "getting" and intellectual "getting"
—the senses get, not the tree, but a sense *form* of this
tree; and memory which is a knowledge power can
retain that form, so that in my mind's eye, I can in
the absence of the tree 'see' the tree. It seems that in
a short time we are enabled to go around possessed
of a host of such sense forms. Mind or intellect does
not stop there; rather it starts there. Working on the
naturally particular sense form of tree X and of tree
Y and of tree Z, it is able to "grasp" the being-meaning-essence of "tree," of any tree and all trees. Then
it can go on and get the being-meaning-essence, in
some disembodied "intentional" way, out of oak X
and oak Y and oak Z. And these beings-meanings-
essences, which of course remain in trees X, Y, and Z
and in oaks X, Y, and Z, are somehow assimilated to
and made one with the knowing mind.

That is something of what Aristotle says about what it means for a man "to know." He says, too, that knowing is a proper excellence and perfection of man, so that a man not knowing would be shortchanged and his condition would be an evil one, the evil usually called ignorance.

Now would ignorance in a Christian differ in any way from ignorance in a non-Christian, and would knowing in a Christian differ in any way from knowing in a non-Christian? It would seem that neither would be in any way different. Well, then, take this set of questions. Are the objects available to be known exactly the same for Christian and non-Christian? That is, has the Christian perhaps a better chance to know some objects? Or has the Christian perhaps a chance to know some objects better than the non-Christian can readily know them?

In the attempt to reply to this set of questions, put just now as three, some have deliberately said there is a something that may justifiably be called a "Christian learning." For the last sixty years or so, they have talked of this as a "Christian philosophy." But we hold that the idea, if valid and available, is valid and available for some learnings other than philosophy. We also hold that the idea is used, with all degrees of correctness and incorrectness, on all levels of learning among Christians and orthodox Jews, and both in and out of schools. Let's try to disembody the idea.

Christians and orthodox Jews hold that God has

spoken to man, not only through nature, but in a direct way. Now any knowledge by sense or intellect, by intuition or sensation or reasoning, is a revelation; and those who say that God has directly spoken to man cover the body of things thus spoken by the word "revelation." Aristotle would understand what they mean: a) that the words thus spoken are a source of knowledge, and b) that they are a special source of knowledge. We said that any other knowing is a "revealing," an "unveiling." We get the knowledge naturally; by our natural powers of sense and intellect we are equipped to get it, and we do get it. We see, we inquire, and reason, we do roundabout research, and at length we know. God speaks to us through Moses and John and the Church, and we know. This knowing is like that which we have when we know because someone has told us something. It is like it in this way that both are authority-knowings: we know on a man's word, and we know on God's word. Yet the knowledge plainly is knowledge, and not mere belief, opinion, or hypothesis.

On the supposition that there is such a direct from-God-to-man knowledge, the masses of people, left to themselves, will take natural knowledge and "not-natural" knowledge pretty much as one thing, just as they bother little to distinguish between sense knowledge and intellectual knowledge. Fine points are not their business. But scholars must always try to distinguish the sources of knowledge, the types of knowledge, the degrees of knowledge, and the objects of knowledge. This will be quite an assignment which perhaps men will never completely and perfectly fulfill. Among the best of scholars, confusions and conundrums will reappear.

The problem of a possible Christian learning comes up within the problem of the interrelationships between common natural knowledge and divinely-directly revealed knowledge. The answers historically and currently suggested to the problem are several and are very interesting. One answer is the ordinary Protestant answer which in effect says there is no relation, for the reason that Revelation is a ground of belief, but not of knowledge. A second answer is a bit like that; it says that there is no relation except that each is a valid kind of knowledge. Oddly enough, this is the answer ordinarily given by American Catholics who are scholars: natural knowledge must stand outside all causal relation to revealed knowledge. I do not mean that men consciously hold and explicitly state this view; many do hold it, however, in an implicit and effective way. What these scholars are assuming is that the two worlds of natural knowledge and revealed knowledge are to be kept iron-curtained off from each other.

One of these worlds would be whatever the Bible, the Church, and theology assure us is true. The other would be whatever knowledge—and this is the knowledge gained by philosophy, science, and common sense—we reach by sense experience and intellectual intuitions and reasoning. There would be no communication between the two, between biblical knowledge and empirically verifiable knowledge, if the Catholic, as is sometimes the case, is a positivist.

On this view, man knowing many things on the natural level knows them only because his senses and intellect grasp them. On that level he cannot: a) know anything because it is divinely-directly revealed; or, b) know anything better—always on that level—because it is divinely-directly revealed; or, c) have a better chance to know anything on that level because it is so revealed.

However, some holding that there is no relation except that each knowledge is a knowledge do say that because of divine-direct revelation we know that some things are not true. They then say that on some matters Revelation is a "negative norm." Does revelation help us in any way to a positive natural knowledge of anything, e.g., in philosophy or sociology? The persons we speak of demand a clean break between the two types of knowledge. They say that it helps us to none and can help us to none.

On this view, then, divine-direct revelation affords quite genuine knowledge, a rich and abundant knowledge. This knowledge put into form is called "theology" just as it is with people of all other views. But on the view under consideration, theology as knowledge, though itself a wonderfully rich knowledge, lies

forever fallow alongside other knowledge. That is
what it has to do. What we know on God's word to
be true can be systematized into a science called
"theology," but can never enrich any other science
or direct the mind to it.

Let us put the matter this way. Just as divine-direct
revelation never helps my eyes to see a rock or a
mountain or my ears to hear a bell ringing, so it never
helps my intellect to reach a natural understanding of
anything.

We might call that view the "revealed-knowl-
edge-only theory," and the Protestant view the "no-
knowledge, faith-only theory." The early Protestant
opinion was that "faith" is in one compartment and
"works" in quite another, and the two shall never
get together on anything. The "revealed-knowledge-
only" theory is like the Protestant view. Revealed
knowledge here, and natural knowledge there, and
the two shall never meet: that sums up the theory
under consideration. No commerce between them.
On the Protestant view, the believer believes hard, and
perhaps he studies and knows just as hard, but all
knowledge in its essence is natural and secular, since
revelation is a source of belief and not of knowledge.
On the presently considered view, a man knows in
two ways, but any knowledge gained in one way is
completely shut off from knowledge gained in the
other way; any knowledge not divinely-directly revealed is and has to be natural and secular.

Theories of a "Christian school" and of a "Christian scholar," based on such different views of the interrelations of revealed knowledge and natural knowledge, are of course fundamentally at odds. A third view of the interrelations, to be stated in a moment, affords yet another theory of what "Christian school" and "Christian scholar" are. These consequent disparate views of Christian school and Christian scholar will be examined in a later chapter.

The third view of how the two knowledges are related is also of much interest. We may begin to look at it in the form of the following problem. Granting that we achieve natural knowledge, I wonder whether divinely-directly revealed knowledge could ever in any way impregnate and fecundate natural knowledge. Could it perhaps help us to know in philosophy or elsewhere something that otherwise we would scarcely know? Or could it perhaps help us to know better what we would know in any case? If we do know—I mean naturally know—anything better because we are gifted with divinely-directly revealed knowledge, then, so far, there is a positive relation between the two types of knowledge, and the two are not forever shelved in different worlds. Again, if we do perhaps know—naturally know—anything at all outright—not merely better, but outright—because of revelation, then again the two worlds approach each other, and at this one point touch. Or even if we have a better chance to know some one

thing, or to know it better, because there is a divinely-
directly revealed knowledge, then, so far, there is a
positive relation between the types and a possible relation of collaboration.

To bring out this third view of the interrelation,
let us take some examples of what the view might add
up to in philosophy and social sciences, and also in
the matter, even the naturally known matter, that an
artist such as poet or painter expresses in his art. Take,
first, the great problem of some direction and meaning in the given universe of nature, or no direction
and meaning in that universe. As Plato made evident
in the *Timaeus*, this is a problem in its nature both
difficult and comprehensive, because it covers all nature, even man as something given in the universe,
and its breakdowns descend to any and all of the physical, biological, moral, and spiritual details. Now it
can be made clear from natural intuitions and reasonings—which of course are philosophy's realm—that
the biological unit has direction and meaning, that the
whole biological world has direction and meaning,
and that particular biological powers and operations,
e.g., the power-operation of seeing or of reproducing,
have direction and meaning; and even that the cosmos
in its entirety is not without direction and meaning.
It can be made clear, and Plato and Aristotle made it
fairly clear.

Of course the science based properly on God's
word is theology, and a science with such basis can

never be made to do duty for philosophy, or vice versa. Theology is theology, with its own bases, assurances, and methods; and philosophy remains philosophy, with its own bases, assurances, and methods. But a philosopher who as a believer has assurance on God's word in regard to direction and meaning, is more likely to be daring and uninhibited enough to go the whole way and arrive, with even more assurance than did Plato and Aristotle, at the philosophical conclusion that nature has direction and meaning. People may ask, "How can this be"—but we may better ask, "How can this not be?" For if God tells us that creation has occurred and that all things, even the lilies of the field and the hairs of our heads come within divine consideration, then we know these matters on God's word. By His word, God gives our minds orientation on the matter. This orientation need not destroy our natural knowledge, or the possibility of it; on the contrary, it may boost and possibly assist natural knowledge, and assist it in its very character of natural knowledge.

The two knowledges, however, are not the same and cannot become the same. The object known is the same. The ways of knowing are not the same. Let us put the case at a minimum. Knowing on God's word that there is direction and meaning in the universe, I will have a better chance, other things being equal, to reach a philosophical and quite natural knowledge of the same truth. Shear the case more closely: perhaps I will have a better knowledge to know that truth or some aspect of it. A Plato or an Aristotle knows this truth of direction and meaning, but a Christian Plato such as Augustine or a Christian Aristotle such as Aquinas would have a better chance to grasp it in its general sweep and in its details.

As a rule, mankind is possessed of that central philosophical truth, held unconsciously and vaguely; but men in the Jewish-Christian tradition have more fully and firmly possessed it. The contrast is the point. Perhaps anybody can "see" that nature has direction and meaning, but to such a philosophy as "naturalism" in twentieth century America, drained rather dry of knowledge held on God's word, it becomes harder to "see" direction and meaning. This is so much the case that when at the end of World War II, Professor Gotshalk of Illinois University said that naturalistic philosophers were hurting themselves by refusing direction and "teleology" in nature, he caused a stir. His point was that direction and end-seeking are fairly obvious, and yet men had been failing to see them. Of course in a society that has long been at least relatively Christian, those who perhaps think they are atheist or agnostic are nevertheless influenced and directed in various ways and degrees, in their philosophical and in their sociological views, by revealed knowledge.

We want to take next an example where philosophical knowledge is enriched, and perhaps enfeoffed, by divinely revealed knowledge. This is the matter of accepting "nature." This is simple: we do accept nature all the time—it is wished on us. Yet the freak thing is that the "naturalistic" philosopher and sociologist, common today in America, have a hard time to accept it. Our "naturalism" rejects revealed knowledge and rejects God, and as a rule rejects spirit. Such "naturalism" was basic in Dewey, and anyone would swear in advance that Dewey, so fond of the word "nature," would declare for nature in man. It is not clear, however, that he did so. For if "nature" is, as we are supposing, determinate being—not just any indeterminate being, which by the way does not exist —and a corresponding determinate tendency to corresponding results, and if any real being such as a man or a crocodile has such being and tendency and ends, then Dewey refused "nature." But so did Kant whose Christianity we believe was real though cramped and unfree: Kant said that he threw "natural tendencies" out of his ethics, and spurned what the sciences of man, which he rightly called anthropology, could tell us about man. Reinhold Niebuhr, one of the best Protestant philosophers in America, is in this regard like Kant: he says that nature is not to be honored and followed, but to be "indeterminately" transcended. Sartre, too, an arbitrary and extreme man, says "there is no human nature."

In the case of Protestants and of lapsed Protestants like Dewey, we think this fear of "nature" as law for man comes from misreading the Bible; that is, from the notion that since the Fall of man, "nature" in man is evil.

Without revelation, man can come to a true understanding of nature and of man's nature, and also of direction and tendency in nature. This understanding can be philosophy—squared with reality, truth reached by natural intuitions and reasonings. But given revelation on the same matters, man has a better chance to arrive at a philosophy of them.

Since the illustrations just covered are difficult, we are going to take some practical issues. The pagan can know chastity as a virtue, but it is more difficult for him to come to a natural philosophical grasp of it as a virtue than it is for a Christian. Knowing from the Bible that chastity is a virtue and living the life of chastity as well as he can—which may be very well indeed—the Christian has a much better chance to reach a natural understanding that chastity is a virtue. Sir Richard Livingstone shows [1] that Plato and Aristotle knew that humility is a virtue. But a natural philosophical understanding of humility as a virtue is more difficult for a pagan and for his civilization than for a Christian and his civilization. So, and more obviously, for sacrifice and suffering; even the unlettered Christian has natural if perhaps "notional" knowledge that these need not be evil, a truth undecipherable to

[1] Sir Richard Livingstone, *Education and the Spirit of the Age* (New York: Oxford University Press, 1952), pp. 55–56.

Aristotle, though as a great biologist and philosopher he was in important ways equipped to get it. Again, the truth that we are to love all, a truth accessible to psychology, sociology, and ethics, is difficult for Christians, but far more so for pagans. "Love men while you have to kill them in a war" contains a truth so hard to get that we should hardly ask Christian soldiers to consider it; yet the Christian sociologist and patriot, Luigi Sturzo, could honestly appeal to it during World War II against the propagandist Rex Stout who could only say, "Hate or you shall fail."

To remain in concrete matters of our century, take contrasted attitudes toward terrible events. Take John Gunther's attitude when his son John suffered and died of brain cancer, and the attitude of William Allen White when his daughter Mary was struck and killed, and the attitude also of the community of each man. Though far from irreverence, Gunther was a secularist-naturalist and the most that he and his community could say was that the dead child belonged to "the continuity of the universe," whereas for White and his community—mostly believing Protestant—the event was tempered by the belief-knowledge that, in the words of the funeral Mass, life was "changed and not wiped out."

What then does this "Christian education" and "Christian learning" finally add up to? What difference does it make? Quite a difference to philosophy, and to sociology, and to a man's or a community's or even a civilization's psychological grasp of things, of man, of good and evil, of "meaning" and "sense" in the universe, of nature itself. We are naive if we think —and some Christians do think it—that God's word on things and on man makes no difference to what we know and to what we advisedly teach in sociology or in political science. The Christian knows some of these matters on theological grounds, and because he does, he and his civilization can outrun the pagan and his civilization in the chance to know them on psychological, sociological, and philosophical grounds, which in a way are the pagan's own grounds.

We have been attempting to state what is meant by saying, as men holding the third view of "Christian knowledge" say, that there is a positive influence of some matters known through God's word on the same matters naturally known. The most famous of all examples is the one often adduced. It is this: After God revealed to Moses and thereby to mankind the nature of God, in the declaration I AM WHO AM, we are better able to know philosophically and naturally what the nature of God is. We know philosophically and naturally that God is pure being and that God's essence and existence are identical; we know that in one being, but only in one being, essence and existence are and must be identical. This is a difficult doctrine, but Jewish and Christian philosophers, given the revealed knowledge that it is true, are able philosophically and naturally to prove it.

If these philosophers can prove the point, pagan philosophers can prove it. This is because what is available to philosophy, is available to philosophy no matter who the philosopher may be. But it would seem that the nonpagan philosopher has a better chance to come to a philosophical knowledge of some things.

Our hypothesis was this: If anything is known philosophically and naturally because it was first known as divinely-directly revealed; or if the philosopher has a better chance, given that background, to know some things precisely as a philosopher, then there would seem so far to be something which we may call a "Christian philosophy." But as our examples indicated, there seem to be matters which men have a better chance to know, given that basis, and things that Christians and Jews do in fact better know. We seem compelled then to say one or two or all of these things; that we know them outright, whereas the pagan does not know them; or we know them better; or at least that we have a better chance to know some of them.

The words we use for the resultant are "Christian philosophy," a controversial and readily ambiguous term. But let us not squabble over matters of words and semantics. If the resultant accrues, we must accept it. If the thing we speak of exists—and we think it has existed, does now exist and will go on dynamically existing—we ought to accept it and see where it leads. Instead of using a roundabout description, covering several pages, it would be handy to have a word or two such as "Christian philosophy" to name it. Besides, we have suggested that "Christian" applies in at least some other fields, so that we are justified in speaking of a "Christian learning."

One difficulty blocking the acceptance of what we have described as "Christian philosophy" comes from a literal and simple formalism. It runs into formulas such as these: If I possess knowledge of something by faith-knowledge, I cannot also know it by natural intuitions and reasonings. Again: Theology as a science is based on the word of God and Church teaching, and philosophy is based on natural intuitions and reasonings; and therefore man cannot learn anything in philosophy from the Bible and theology and Church teaching.

The difficulty is simplistic and over-formal, and in some Catholics it arises from their having studied in seminaries where the study of philosophy, at least in this country, is extremely formalistic and, like Kant's philosophy, far from the empiric realities of science and history. But let us not damn it with the words "formal" and "Kantian." Let us be realistic and say that it is not only in philosophy that we know many things before we have anything except authority as our reason for affirming them. Everybody does the same thing in science and in common sense knowledge. I know, but only on authority, that Scotland exists, and perhaps sometime I shall get other proofs of it. I know, but only on people's word, that Eisenhower had a heart attack in 1955; but perhaps it may be possible for me to have other proofs of it.

So, too, in science. We know many things on the authority of parents, teachers and doctors; and perhaps some day we will get other than authority proofs of them. That is the way the budding scientist learns —first, on the basis of authority, then on the basis of firsthand proofs, a fact put so far beyond cavil by Dr. Polanyi that we are happy to use his remarkable statement. Dr. Polanyi says that in its effort to learn to speak, the child is led forward by the conviction that speech means something, a point which the child is yet in no position to prove. The child is guided by his parents and "perceives the light of reason in their eyes, voice and bearing and feels instinctively attracted towards the source of this light." Dr. Polanyi proceeds:

Apprenticeship to the higher arts, and to science in particular, is accepted and pursued on similar grounds. The future scientist is attracted by popular literature or by schoolwork in science long before he can form any true idea of the nature of scientific research. The morsels of science which he picks up—even though often dry or else speciously varnished—instil in him the intimation of intellectual treasures and creative joys far beyond his ken. His intuitive realization of a great system of valid thought and of an endless path of discovery sustains him in laboriously accumulating knowledge and urge him on to penetrate into intricate brain-racking theories. Sometimes he will find a master whose work he admires and whose manner and outlook he accepts for his guidance. Thus his mind will become assimilated to the premisses of science. The scientific intuition of reality henceforth shapes his perception. He learns the methods of scientific investigation and accepts the standards of scientific value.

At every stage of his progress towards this end he is urged on by the belief that certain things as yet beyond his knowledge and even understanding are on the whole true and valuable. This represents a recognition of the authority of that which he is going to learn and of those from whom he is going to learn it. It is the same attitude as that of the child listening to its mother's voice and absorbing the meaning of speech. Both are based on an implicit belief in the significance and truth of the context which the learner is trying to master. . . . No one can become a scientist unless he presumes that the scientific doctrine and method are fundamentally sound and that their ultimate premisses can be unquestionably accepted.[1]

What is perhaps most remarkable about Dr. Polanyi's statement is the conclusion immediately following the lines just quoted. Dr. Polanyi goes on

[1] Michael Polanyi, *Science, Faith and Society* (New York: Oxford University Press, 1946), pp. 30–31, 69–70.

in his sane and simple manner to say that the first step of the child toward skills and science is based on belief-knowledge or what may be called authority-knowledge: the child, not yet proving that X is true, knows that it is true: he takes the word of Einstein or of his parents. "We have here," says Polanyi, "an instance of the process described epigrammatically by the Christian Church Fathers in the words: *fides quaerens intellectum*, faith in search of understanding."

Let us try to get a better picture of the process reported in this famous if cryptic formula, and let us add its fellow formula, *Credo ut intelligam*. These formulas sum up the thought of generations and also sum up what we have said in expressing the third view of the relation of knowledge based directly on God's word to knowledge based properly on natural intuitions and reasonings. In this chapter we have been mainly engaged in trying to state the relation of Christian theology to what we have called "Christian philosophy." But we are always aware of two problems: first, the relation of this theology to any conceivable "Christian learnings" in any other fields; and secondly, the problem of whether the knower in any field, say of social science or of physical science, can proceed on an entirely "value-free" assumption; in particular on the assumption that knowledge itself is not a value and is not a good and end that the scientist, here and now in his science, is seeking. For our part, we are sure that knowledge, whatever its source and type, is an end or value both worthy of being sought by man and in fact being sought by him.

Now for the "fides-intellectum" and the "credo-intelligam" formulas. The latter formula is literally translated as, "I believe in order to understand." The historic and real sense of it, put at a minimum, is this: Knowing X, Y, and Z on the ground of God's word, I will perhaps have a better chance to reach a philosophical, natural intuition-reasoning knowledge of X, Y, and Z than if I had not known them on the ground of God's word.

Just as by belief-knowledge on Einstein's word that M is true does not destroy or invalidate forever my chance to know scientifically that M is true, but increases my chance to know that M is true, so my belief-knowledge, based on God's word, that X, Y, and Z are true does not destroy or invalidate my chance to know philosophically that they are true, but increases my chance to know that they are true.

For one thing, belief-knowledge on Einstein's word or on God's word sets the human mind off: the mind wants to know now, not merely on man's or God's word, but by way of scientific or philosophical proof. This fact is covered by the other formula, *fides quaerens intellectum:* faith-knowledge tends to seek scientific and philosophical knowledge. That is the way the human mind works, says Dr. Polanyi; if we did not go for science and philosophy in that faith-knowledge way, we should be extremely unlikely to go for them at all; every child would have to begin without any tutoring from God or the human race, and all by himself learn whatever he would be able to learn. Accumulated knowledge could mean nothing. According to the old "radical empiricism" of William James, as well as the logical positivism of today, the human mind can validly know, in philosophy and sociology, only by junking the method by which in fact it does know, the method of first knowing, on the word of God, parents, teachers, and scientists, and then arriving at other bases for knowing.

Fortunately, that radically empiric and positivist way is not the way the human mind needs to work or commonly does work. The mind of each child, as we come one by one to knowledge, is not left thus stranded, a completely disinherited Crusoe.

» 3 «

Witnesses

AMONG central points and theses of this book, two
are being carried from cover to cover. The first,
stated in chapter one, is that schools founded and
conducted for intellectual ends are much more likely
to reach those ends than institutions set up and operated for other ends, such as military, political, religious, or financial. This is evident, and it is a point
that has something to say about the evolution and
status of American Catholic schools.

The other point has just been roughed out in chapter two. It is that a "Christian philosophy" and a
"Christian learning" seem to be good enough captions
under which to express the relation between Christian
theological learning, based immediately on divinely-
directly revealed truth, and any and all natural learning, that is to say a learning based on nature. We were
there saying for instance that Jews and Christians,

having directly from God the truth-rightness of the Ten Commandments, might have a better chance to get a natural grasp of the truth-rightness of the Commandments, a better chance to see them in all their ethical and sociological implications, than a people not knowing their truth-rightness on God's word. The truth-rightness of the Commandments and the ethical and sociological implications of them can ideally be arrived at by any people. But which people can arrive there more surely—the Jewish-Christian people, or a pagan people?

We say the former can. If so, they are more capable —not absolutely, but in the circumstances—than a pagan people of arriving at truths naturally accessible to all.

In that case there would be possible a "Christian philosophy" and a "Christian sociology," and so far there would be possible a "Christian learning." The world so understood would then be standard material for Christians who are artists. But beyond that point has a Christian learning conceivably any farther possibilities? Perhaps so, and perhaps not. Perhaps not a speck of it is possible in any sense in the understanding of history or in biological or physical or mathematical sciences. This is a complex and difficult problem with which we do not choose to wrestle.

At the end of chapter two we said that some persons, touched by a sort of Kantian formalism, cannot see our second point, and are left with an unhistorical and unreal gap between learning directly revealed and any learning—to use St. Paul's formulation (Romans, chap. 1)—not directly revealed.

Another reason for the nonacceptance of the idea of "Christian learning" will now be mentioned, a reason much more influential and affecting men of importance in many fields of learning. Let us remark that this reason ties in with the origins of the American Catholic school system, which we saw was founded to save the faith and morals of students, but soon acquired a second nonintellectual cause for being: it became an apologist for the faith. It aimed not only to save the faith in children, it aimed to make the faith look good to adult outsiders. That "look good to outsiders" idea is also a dominating idea with many Catholics who are heads of colleges and universities, and even with some distinguished Catholics who are scholars. Of course, that idea as a dominating idea is wider and older than America. It is a heritage of the Reformation and of centuries during which Catholics suffered a state of siege. We may be sure it affects Protestants, too, especially in nations where they are in the minority. In America it affects Catholics who, quite in the minority, want to look good to the more or less ruling majority. This idea also combines with a propaganda idea: learning is good both because it defends the faith, making it look good, and because it helps to propagate the faith.

We have long lived with college and university

people, and have noticed that priests are affected more than others by this idea of learning, this idea of "defend the faith, spread the faith." Priests readily adopt this apologetic-propaganda end as the end of learning, and some lay Catholics who are scholars, even well established scholars in high places in non-Catholic universities, are greatly affected by this motive of "save the faith, spread the faith." That becomes the end and purpose of learning.

Some of these remarkable scholars scarcely leave themselves free to pursue learning with the gay abandon of children playing. They find it foreign to pursue learning—"Christian learning" included—let the apologetic and propaganda chips fall where they may. They do of course love and pursue learning, but are a trifle overawed by what the gentiles will think. If the Christian is a great scholar, surely the gentile, otherwise looking on suspiciously, will be pleased,—one might say, appeased and placated. And so, in order that the gentile will not be displeased, the Christian who is a scholar must be wary: he must take the gentile's view of the relation between divinely-directly revealed knowledge and knowledge not divinely-directly revealed. If the gentile doctor honors the former at all, his position is that it is to be held forever incommunicado in relation to the latter. It would offend him no end if we were to say there is a "Christian learning" in any sense or measure, outside the directly revealed learning of the Bible.

Therefore, for this apologetic-propaganda reason, it must be held that there is no Christian learning. At least it must never be said that there is such a learning, and people do not then feel free to raise the question whether there may be this type of learning. "I can think of scholars who would be grieved to hear it if there is such a Christian learning." So said a Catholic of distinction who is a scholar of distinction. Think of a scholar not leaving himself free to inquire, to investigate, and to know, and to declare.

This type of apologetic stance is sure to affect a minority group naturally tending to be on the defensive, and to affect it in matters other than academic. But the psychology of it is unfortunate. It does some harm to academic people who are thereby rendered less free to investigate and inquire and to let the facts lead where they may.

Before we proceed, let us add some common reasons why good men are slow to go with the idea of a "Christian philosophy" and a "Christian learning." We have seen two of the reasons: some are frightened off by the formal, quasi-Kantian notion that, since theology is based on the Bible and Church teaching, and philosophy is based on natural intuitions and reason, philosophy can get no leads or aid or comfort from the Bible and Church teachings; and the mere fact that historically philosophy has taken such leads and profited as philosophy by them is not enough to swing the scales in favor of its being able to do so.

The other reason, adduced in the last couple of pages, though it affects more persons and persons who are more scholarly, is the shabbier of the two. The one mentioned first is formal and Kantian and says that though a thing has happened and keeps happening, it cannot happen. The second says, "What a shame it would be if this 'Christian philosophy' and 'Christian learning' thing was found to be true! What a fix we would be in! Secularist scholars would frown on us and say that we are dogmatic and not scholars."

A third reason for rejecting the notion of Christian learning is that it is a considerable and comprehensive idea; it is difficult in any case to grasp, and above all in a world where for formal-Kantian and apologetic reasons we have been afraid of the idea. To grasp it is difficult, and to carry it through, applying it to many learnings, is difficult; just as, of course, it is difficult to grasp any central, underlying, and unifying idea in educational philosophy and difficult to apply it in various fields of learning.

To get help in clarifying the idea of Christian learning we are going to call on the strongest men available—Etienne Gilson, Jacques Maritain, and Dietrich von Hildebrand. These men are experts on Christian philosophy and Christian learning and by reviewing their teachings on the matter we will be able to see those ideas from new and luminous points of view, though since their precision statements are slightly technical and since we have said in chapter two what we take Christian learning to be, some may choose to skip to the end of the present chapter.

For forty years, Gilson has been hot as a fire-cracker on the subject, convinced that the idea of Christian philosophy is true and that it is important for both the thinking and the practical life of man-kind. At first, Gilson went somewhat out of his way —as we did in the preceding chapter—to show against the Kantian-formalist mind that there is nothing in-herently out of line in the idea of "Christian phi-losophy." There his argument holds up well; and then it gets tremendous added force as Gilson pro-ceeds. For he has spent his life in showing that what he calls a "Christian philosophy" has in fact existed and developed throughout centuries. From history he takes great witnesses, from among whom it is enough for us to name two of his saints, Anselm and Augus-tine. From Anselm he lifts the famous formula, *fides quaerens intellectum:* that is, faith-knowledge is seek-ing to become a philosophical knowledge; or as Gilson says, for generations people were trying to convert truths believed into truths known. The relevance of Augustine is dual: he too had the idea of a Christian philosophy, in fact the same idea of it that Gilson has, and at the same time he was one of the great-est Christian philosophers. And Augustine had a formula right out of the Bible to say the thing. The version of Isaias (7:9) used by Augustine reads, *Nisi credideritis non intelligetis:* "Unless you had believed, you would not have understood." Hence Augustine can be seen to put matters more vigorously than our chapter did. We only said that having belief-knowledge you will have or perhaps you will have a better chance to arrive at the other knowledge. Augustine says that unless you first have the one, you will not have the other.

Gilson proceeds: "Thus the content of Christian philosophy is that body of rational truths discovered, explored or simply safeguarded, thanks to the help that reason receives from revelation." This would cover the matter or content, but Gilson goes on to designate—not, of course, to try to define—a "Christian philosophy": "Thus I call Christian, *every philosophy which, although keeping the two orders formally distinct, nevertheless considers Christian revelation as an indispensable auxiliary to reason.*" [1]

The best of all brief passages to show how scholars for centuries conceived and used the idea of "Christian philosophy" is itself a prayer. Duns Scotus (d. 1308) was setting out to write a book on God [2] and it came at once to Scotus—it was stock in trade with him and his times—that what God tells us in the Bible about what God is, about the nature of God, is

[1] We are using Gilson's *The Spirit of Mediaeval Philosophy,* Tr. by A. H. C. Downes (New York: Sheed & Ward, 1936), chap. 2. Gilson has said the same thing in a variety of ways and in many volumes.

[2] See Gilson, *op. cit.,* pp. 51–52.

exactly what we want to arrive at in our philosophical understanding of God. It did not occur to Scotus, a man equipped with faith-knowledge, to proceed in any other way. We call his prayer the prayer of the Christian philosopher, and we see at once that his prayer or one like it should be the prayer used by Christian teachers and students as they undertake their professional tasks. Here is the prayer:

O Lord our God, when Moses asked of Thee as the most true teacher, by what name he should name Thee to the people of Israel; knowing well what mortal understanding could conceive of Thee and unveiling to him Thy ever blessed name, Thou didst reply: *Ego sum qui sum.* Wherefore Thou art true being, total being. This I believe, but if it be in any way possible this I would also know. Help me, O Lord, to seek out such knowledge of the true being that Thou art as may lie within the power of my natural reason, starting from that being which Thou Thyself has attributed to Thyself.

That, then, is Gilson on the relation of Christian theology and the Bible to a possible Christian philosophy. The former gives to the latter some of the latter's content. Philosophy if it is to be philosophy must be kept *formaliter* distinct from theology; yet philosophy is not debarred from obtaining from theology some notion of where some truths lie. If those truths are ever to be philosophically known, they must be philosophically proved. It is the case all over again of the youthful scientist who has on Einstein's word some belief-knowledge, and in that way knows some things; but he has not scientific knowledge of those things. If he is some day to have a scientific knowledge, he must work it out scientifically and not suppose he can have it on Einstein's word, though this word sets him out on the road to obtain it.

Philosophical knowledge is to be kept "formally distinct" from theological knowledge. How distinct is that? As distinct as soul from body; soul is not body, nor vice versa, and one can never serve as the other; but soul and body are not separated. The penalty for separation is death. The same holds for the separation of theology and philosophy: distinct, yes; separated, no. Gilson and others have always been saying that the separation of these disciplines which ought not to be separated but only to be kept distinct is the greatest error in Descartes.

On occasion, too, Gilson has suggested a wider application of his central idea. Let us put this question: If there is anything to the notion that a Christian philosophy is possible or even actual, is it conceivable that "Christian" could make sense when applied to some other fields of learning? Is its whole extension exhausted once we have applied the idea in philosophy?

It is obvious that a science based on truths divinely-directly revealed, is in important senses the highest science. It has God as object of its knowledge, and God also as the source of this knowledge; other sciences and arts are subordinate to it. None of them has God as the direct source of its knowledge, though some may have God as object of their knowledge. But to say that, because all other knowledges are thus subordinate to theology, therefore theology is the ordering and integrating science is a simple mistake; the mistake comes from the ambiguity of "subordinate to" and "ordered by." We need to get this confusion out of our heads in American Catholic schools. Merely because other knowledges are in some real sense *sub*-ordered to theology, we may not therefore say that theology is the ordering and integrating principle, and that all other knowledges are ordered and integrated by it.

The science that understands order itself is metaphysics; and the ordering principle, incorrectly called the "integrating" principle, is a principle drawn from metaphysics. Of course "metaphysics" is one of the sciences to be ordered; and the formal, ordering principle drawn from metaphysics is, as St. Thomas often says, the *ratio ordinis:* it is the basic formal principle. This principle is *the* principle of order, and—like the last end—is a *ne plus ultra:* in its realm, it is the last word.

That is what we take Gilson, and all medieval and

modern doctors, to mean when they say that theology is the highest of the sciences. Their position in this regard calls for no long discussion.

Gilson goes much farther [1] and suggests outlines within which the savant, whatever his specialty, can be a Christian savant. The savant or learned man must honor the relation of his science to theology— that goes without saying. But, then, if as savant he has it in his head to be an apologist for the Church, he must first of all be an excellent savant "and not merely an intelligent and cultivated man more or less anointed by science. If one wishes to practice science for God, the first condition is to practice science for itself, or as if one practiced it for itself, for that is the only way of acquiring it. . . . He is bound by the very intention which guides him, to become a good savant, a good philosopher or a good artist." Piety must not be substituted for knowledge; piety never dispenses with technique.

Whatever their faith or lack of faith in God and revelation, all savants are bound to be excellent savants. The Christian savant has to go farther. As others, he works to understand and express nature. But the Christian has the belief-knowledge that nature is the handiwork of God and that the better he knows nature the better he knows God. The savant

[1] Etienne Gilson, *Christianity and Philosophy* (New York and London: Sheed & Ward, 1939), chap. 5, "The Intelligence in the Service of Christ the King."

goes beyond apologetics and studies the sciences "against no one, but for God." Still, continues Gilson, "to serve God by science or art, it is necessary to begin by practicing them *as if* these disciplines were in themselves their own ends": which in a sense they truly are, even if in another sense they are means. As men of learning, what we must keep in mind is that it is impossible to place the intelligence at God's service "without respecting integrally the rights of the intelligence." Otherwise, "it would not be the intelligence that is put at His service."

"Getting reason to guide itself by faith"—this is perhaps the best formula in Gilson for the over-all relation between theology and other knowledges. He has emphasized a positive relation; we wish that he had somewhere attempted to express further just how some art or science other than philosophy is affected by standing in that relation.

Jacques Maritain, friend of Gilson's, has perhaps above all others in North America stood for the idea and the fact of Christian philosophy. He says [1] that "Christian philosophy" is not a nature or essence, it is not a species of philosophy as a horse is a species of animal. It is philosophy in a particular state or condition. In reviewing Maritain's way of saying this, we find it better to speak of the "Christian philoso-

[1] See especially Maritain's *An Essay on Christian Philosophy*, Tr. by Edward Flannery (New York: Philosophical Library, 1955), pp. ix–xi, 3–33.

pher." This person is a philosopher, who therefore, according to Maritain, begins with experience and then using natural intuitions and reasonings proceeds to such theoretic and practical wisdom as he can reach. But as Christian philosopher, one does not proceed in "just any old" conditions, since no real being exists in such impossible conditions. A real being exists and operates in particular conditions; and so of course does the Christian philosopher.

Now a man operating, not in a vacuum, but in particular conditions is advantaged and disadvantaged in many ways by these conditions. Maritain holds that operating in the general way describable as "Christian" is a great advantage to men as philosophers, and can be a real advantage to men of learning in some other fields. Let us see how he details the advantage. First of all, there are objective data, matters possessed at the outset by the philosophizing man on the basis of belief-knowledge. Maritain names four truths thus given: the idea of *creation;* the idea of *nature not absolutely closed* upon itself, but open to a supernatural order; the idea of *God as subsisting being itself;* and the idea of *sin as an offense against God,* "an idea of which in spite of manifold attempts Western philosophy has not managed to rid itself."

Ideas such as these are of paramount importance for the whole of philosophy, and in regard to each of these ideas "reason has unquestionably received a positive endowment. . . . The moment philosophy is advised of these elements it scrutinizes them according to its own order, which *ascends* from experience toward things divine (whereas revelation *descends* from God)."

Let us suppose that some truths revealed by God are nevertheless truths we can know in the natural order. The fact is that powerful pagan minds, though not in sheer and total night in relation to such truths, were either at a standstill or went astray. Christians need not, however, claim that as philosophers they perfectly grasp all the loftiest truths. "The question at issue here is rather concerned—and this is still of paramount importance—with differences of clarity that are, to tell the truth, extraordinarily pronounced": Christian philosophers know some things better than pagan philosophers do. They know things better because they are advantaged to begin with by belief-knowledge. Or, as said in the preceding chapter, they know things the pagan scarcely knows at all.

Besides, philosophy learns something while being led "along paths which are not its own"; by the fact that it is asked, as it is not in a pagan society, to help elucidate Christian mysteries. Philosophy's field of inquiry is thus broadened; as regards sensible objects, philosophy is prudent and humble enough to seek enlightenment from natural sciences; why should it not also learn something of divine things from faith and theology? Again, the philosopher's own personal experience is vitalized by Christianity, because he is offered as a datum a world as the handiwork of the Word wherein everything expresses the infinite Spirit to finite spirits who know themselves as spirits. What a starting point! A fraternal attitude toward reality is engendered. This attitude thus encouraged, says Maritain (along with Whitehead), was seminal for modern science.

It is unrealistic to suppose that only one thing counts in philosophy; namely, the nature of philosophy, and not its state or condition. A man is a man whether slave or free, but his state or condition makes "a whale" of a difference. In the state or condition of which we speak, philosophy is orientated toward a higher wisdom, and in that way is able to achieve self-detachment, and happily is relieved of some of its ponderousness.

But is it philosophy alone and not any other discipline that learns from and is really and positively advantaged by its professors and students being in a Christian condition? On Maritain's view, certainly not. What we wish, however, is what we wished in the case of Gilson, that Maritain would have attempted a considerable detailing of which learnings—say, the social sciences, and such and such arts—are thus advantaged, and how they are advantaged. Fortunately, he does say something on this fundamental question. His words are few, but are so much to the point that we must see how he approaches the little he does say on the subject. He is setting out to state the problem of a possible Christian philosophy and that of a possible wider Christian learning. He has said that the philosopher must fully safeguard the "absolute rigor and special purity" of philosophy, and has just said that there is philosopher and philosopher: one man thinking he should divorce his philosophic labor from the life of prayer, the other joining them in an organic and living unity and quickening his professional efforts by a life of contemplative wisdom. The result in each case will be philosophic wisdom—but with a difference. Hence the problem: Must we say that anything which may justifiably be called "Christian philosophy" is forever inconceivable? Then follow these words of Maritain on a possible like problem in other fields of learning:

"The same problem is encountered again, moreover, though in different terms, in the case of the artist, as also in the case of the historian or the exegete." (Italics ours.)

Before we take up the challenging way in which Dr. von Hildebrand says these same things, we remark (partly on our own) that some of the data furnished by theology and mentioned by Maritain readily make a major difference to learnings other than philosophy. Such notions as these—sin as an offense against God, man's perduring relativity, God loving and to be loved, man himself inviolate, nature itself, above all in man, caught up somehow in transcendent purpose—these and many related notions

can have an immense influence on social life and
therefore on a realistic social science. Take the actual
case mentioned earlier, the doctrine of a journalist-
propagandist holding that for reasons of expediency
man is to be taught to hate the "enemy" he kills in a
war, and the doctrine of a social scientist holding that
in the light of truth and in spite of hysteria, indoctri-
nation and the mores, a man is to love the "enemy" he
is killing in a war. Man is to love all men, or man is
to hate some men—there is a measureless gap between
these doctrines, and the love-doctrine or the hate-
doctrine is fundamental not only for philosophy of
nature and philosophy of conduct, but for theory and
practice in the area of the political life, and for the
whole lively business of peace and war. No doubt the
love-doctrine as well as the hate-doctrine comes from
a particular view of man and his dignity and significance. But the fact that the two views are so dia-
metrically opposed suggests that they have radically
different sources, and a social science inhibited from
examining the fact along with its sources and its implications is hopelessly unrealistic.

In regard to each field of the more human knowledges such as history, poetry, sociology, and philosophy, Maritain's point is that the world of ideas
within which a man lives and works is going to make
a difference to his understanding of things. Maritain's view of the question is what is best called "actual" or "existential," an "existentialist" view meaning

that man as philosopher or poet or sociologist does not live and think in a vacuum, in a mere "essential" realm where only essences count. Man lives and thinks and expresses himself in a world presently and concretely existing.

That is one premise of the argument. The other is that our own concrete given world is in fact, for many a man and for better or worse, laden with belief-knowledges about creation, about sin, about man's dignity and his present and lasting importance. Given these and many other matters of belief-knowledge, a Dante or a Milton has things of his own times and "state or condition" to say, and a Homer, for all his greatness, is not in an "existential" position to say these things. Given Homer's frame of reference, there are things he is indeed likely to say, and things —perhaps true ones at that—which he cannot say; yet these latter, in another frame of reference, are at once accessible to a Dante or a Milton.

If that is true, the content of poetry or of any art is going, as sure as fire, to be affected by the world of given belief-knowledge, pagan or Christian, true or false, in which the poet and artist operate.

In a way, it is a kind of nonsense to speak of a "Catholic poetry" or a "Catholic art." But it is realism to speak of a poet or an artist operating in a particular existential climate, since he can exist only in such a climate. Poetry will remain poetry, and art will remain art, each with its own exigencies. And so of philosophy or sociology and history. Each has its methods and materials, and each remains itself, poetry, or philosophy, or sociology. But the man working in the art or science has his being in a particular climate which can be pagan or Christian or a hybrid between them. The "state" or "condition" of the man working, the given setup which Maritain occasionally calls "climate," is a real historical world sure to leave its mark on what is said by poet or philosopher or anyone else working creatively in an art or a human science. What is known or thought to be known, what is felt and how it is felt—to suppose that all this remains unaffected by the "climate" and "condition" of the worker, and the worker unaffected by that "climate," is to ask man to do his work in a land of pure essences.

That is what we take Maritain to be saying, and this general position, whether affirmed by Maritain or another, is of fundamental importance for philosophy of education, and of course at the same time for the actual operation of schools.

It is perhaps altogether a different question when we leave the knowledge of the most human matters and come to mathematics, physical science, and biological science. Many have said, perhaps glibly, that to speak of "Christian mathematics" is nonsense. So it is, if we are speaking of an essence—speaking in "essentialist" terms. But so is it nonsense to speak of "Christian philosophy" as an essence. On the other

hand, a distinguished mathematician has suggested
that the matters selected to be studied and to be emphasized for example in "cybernetics" might depend
on whether a mathematician is or is not a Christian.
We must waive the point, and in fact the whole issue
as regards mathematics. We waive the issue as regards
physical sciences, too, and are willing to waive it for
the present as regards biology, though one biologist
suggests that theology, at least in the sense of Church
teaching, may sometimes act as a negative norm; e.g.,
in the study of heredity.

Of course, to lay down a universal negative—"No
one, no mathematician ever did or ever will learn
anything in his science because of his existential Christian condition"—this "never-never" sort of proposition is premature and dogmatic.

So much for what we take to be Maritain's position on these issues, and also for the direction in
which we think his suggestion leads when he says
that it is not only the philosopher who has a problem
set by the givenness of belief-knowledge. Others have
a like problem, each in his own terms; for instance,
the poet, the exegete, and the historian.

Next we proceed to see the way the question is
handled by Dr. von Hildebrand. This distinguished
scholar has suffered much for his belief in the person's freedom and human dignity. Though our era is
a strenuous one, he says that it is "more awake, more
restless, more shaken, more apocalyptic, when com-

pared with the complacency of the liberal era, with its humanitarian illusions of the possibility of living a happy and meaningful life without God." What does this man, himself on the apocalyptic side, make of "Catholic" as attached to learning and scholar and school?

For one thing, he says that though nature is knowable and is to be known, the man knowing is relatively capacitated or incapacitated by his over-all general *attitude*. The attitude of the person knowing makes a difference, and a man's native abilities may be more or less immobilized by any of four negative attitudes. First, by indolence of mind: certain things to be known are beyond our ordinary knowledge range; e.g., the nature of person, of value, or of essences, or the existence of spiritual wholes such as "epochs of civilization," or again social organisms and juridical facts. A grasp of such things requires a soaring power of the mind, an anti-indolent willingness to look in a new direction and to "collaborate" with and "conspire" with the object. Second, an incapacity rooted in pride. One won't let things speak, one won't listen; one is cocksure and is trapped by "that pedagogic pedantry" in the face of the world which destroys all mystery and wonder. Third, an incapacity rooted in resentment, rebellion against the autonomy and objectivity of things, an attitude which gives us either the radical skeptic attacked by Plato, or the man who repeats the absolute thesis that all is relative. Last, the attitude of distrust toward things rendering the mind impotent.

A fortunate byproduct of modern research methods is the desire to have knowers on all levels as well as those in research as free, unbiased, unimpassioned, and objective as men can well be. It would be silly to try to find men without attitudes, and it is unreal to suppose that a knower's negative attitudes, his moral make-up, his philosophical outlook and his religious or his *a*religious and anti-religious attitudes have nothing to do with his knowing. The knower is a man; a man has attitudes, and his theory and practice are sure to be influenced by those attitudes.

Now the attitude of the Catholic to the world to be known is ideally a remarkably good one. So says Dr. von Hildebrand who means not an indifferent Catholic, but the person who lives in the world opened to man by revelation and the community of the Church. That man's attitude is precisely the attitude that frees our knowledge—"delivers" it—knocks off fetters and produces the type of mind capable of doing justice to the depth and range of reality. The Catholic attitude is soaring (says the Doctor), it is anti-pedantic, anti-self-complacent, open, filled with respect for being.

"The true Catholic attitude is one of humility, free from all *ressentiment*, ready to submit and to serve; it is metaphysically courageous, healthy, un-disgruntled, *believing*. I say this is the *Catholic attitude, not* the attitude of the average Catholic." Some Catholic men of science and erudition lack this attitude, and in this regard many non-Catholics are more "Catholic" than many Catholics. We find pedantry, smugness, and cocksureness among Catholic men of science; but not because they are Catholic.

Great natural gifts along with disciplined hard work are required for any field of knowledge. Piety is no substitute for such gifts, and in relation to them nothing could be more foolish, says our author, than a sort of sour-grape superiority on the part of Catholics. Catholics who are scholars are required to appreciate and assimilate good work, even (as Pius XII says) if it should come from behind iron curtains. "All I mean, here, is that the right fundamental attitude is an essential and decisive factor; and that, moreover, without it no adequate knowledge is possible, however much other advantages of intelligence, industry, and thoroughness may be present."

On Dr. von Hildebrand's view, why should we have "Catholic schools"? For the reason he has detailed: for the "right fundamental attitude," and for the "adequate" knowledge just now mentioned by him. "For this reason," he says,[1] "the Catholic may

[1] We have throughout used Dietrich von Hildebrand's "Catholicism and Unprejudiced Knowledge," published in his *The New Tower of Babel* (New York: P. J. Kenedy & Sons, 1953), pp. 127–163, though our first quotation was from page four. The same chapter appeared, in almost the same form, as "The Conception of the Catholic University," in *The University in a Changing World*, ed. by Kotschnig (New York: Oxford University Press, 1932).

never artificially divest himself, even in the use of his natural reason, of the attitude that the *lumen supranaturale* imparts to him; on the contrary, for the sake precisely of really unprejudiced, objective knowledge and genuinely scientific work, the Catholic cannot follow too much the guiding influence of Revelation in the formation of his fundamental attitude, cannot be too Catholic. *Catholic universities* are therefore necessary for the sake of truly adequate objective knowledge, not by any means merely for the protection of the religious convictions of the students."

Our next chapter, using materials from the present chapter and its predecessor, sums up divergent meanings of "Catholic learning," and the consequent implied divergent meanings of "Catholic scholar" and "Catholic school."

» 4 «

A "Catholic School"

WHY we should have "Catholic schools" at all is a simple question. At least it looks simple enough. For a moment let us sum up reasons given by some of our neighbors why we should not have them. An obvious argument against them is their cost—they mean duplication, for which Catholic people have to pay; and we can understand that young growing families, with fixed salaries and a staggering overhead, are not anxious to foot the twin bill for tax-supported schools and for schools not tax supported. This reason is a constant, and we may be sure it was advanced a hundred and twenty years ago when American Catholics first began to build parochial schools. It is always a burden to support non-tax-supported schools, it is always "just becoming impossible" to support them, and yet we have done it; and though we cannot build enough of them, we are building schools and we will continue to build them.

A second argument is advanced by non-Catholics and a few half-Catholics. It is that private, non-tax-supported schools are "divisive." What does that mean? It means that the Jones children go to a Catholic school in this block and the Browns to a tax-supported school in the next block. And the Jones kids are not exposed to the same teaching, good or bad, as the Browns are. That is exactly why people want non-tax-supported schools—they want for their children something that good tax-supported schools, as now operated in America, cannot give. Catholic schools certainly are "divisive"—children are coming out of them with something the other children do not get so readily if at all. But is the "divisive" phenomenon so novel? Let us take a look at it. Churches are "divisive"; the Baptist church is divisive, proffering something that the Episcopal does not proffer, and vice versa. Where men are free as in our society, they will decide for themselves which churches they will or will not go to, and which schools they will or will not send their children to. "Variety in unity" and "unity in variety" are of the essence of freedom and democracy.

Some people are by nature levelers. They feel and sometimes say that all must line up—or else! They say that all must go to one type of school and one type of church; all must vote for one man and one party in "free" elections. Some of these levelers are good people, very earnest souls. Just name off some of the best known in America: Dr. James B. Conant, a leveler on secondary education, Mrs. Agnes Meyer, a leveler on all education, Paul Blanshard, a leveler on everything. These souls are good and are as earnest as Hitler, but they tend to be of the dangerous, dictator type, missing as they do something that goes with the nature of democracy, and in fact with the nature of government.[1]

Thus the question, "Why Catholic schools," is in one important sense a part of the wider question, "Why freedom," and of the question, "Why private anything—churches, economy, hospitals, medicine, houses." It is naturally a part also of another wider question, "Why schools."

The "why" of schools is simple. We have schools because we need them, and we have private schools, Catholic or others, because we need them. We also have Catholic and other private schools because we want them, and because, wanting them, we have a natural right to have them, as Justice McReynolds went out of his way to say in the now famous Oregon school case (1925). We already knew this, but it was encouraging to have him and the federal Supreme

[1] Arguing against Plato's case for leveling, Aristotle shows in a famous passage (*Politics*, Book II, chapters 1–5) that to destroy "variety in unity," and thus to destroy freedom, is to destroy the State.

Court unanimously tell us such acceptable matters: that we have a right to private schools, that it is at bottom the parents' and not the State's business to say to which type of school the children are to be sent, and that our philosophy of government unlike (McReynolds said) some other philosophies is so sound and excellent as to back that natural right.

Enough for this part of our problem. The levelers are out, because they are against good government, against rights and freedom, and against American theory and practice. It is all the same whether the levelers demand that all our schools be Catholic or all be Baptist or all be Jewish or all be American public schools or all be Communist schools. In none of these cases are we going to like the levelers.

The reason for maintaining Catholic schools, however, is more particular than the general good of having schools and being free to have them and having a right to have them. The reason is yet more basic: it is that we hope to make available in these schools some particular intellectual values not available in tax-supported schools, good and necessary as these latter are. What these values are depends on what a Catholic school or in general a Christian school ideally is and what it ideally does. But what it is and what it does—well, these are complicated questions, and though in practice we find much agreement, we also find disagreement on how to answer them.

A first answer is this, if we may be so bold as to

try to suggest the Protestant reply. Falling out long ago over which shade of Protestantism—traditional or modernist—should be taught in American public schools, Protestants then declared for neutral, secularized, *a*religious schools,—not of course that they wanted these, though unhappily their action presupposed them and precipitated them.[1] This effect followed above all, and in fact almost exclusively, on the primary and secondary levels. Everybody now finds the results to be decidedly mixed—satisfactory and unsatisfactory; but it is rather late to change the situation, and we find very few, and these mainly Lutherans and Episcopalians, facing up to the problem of doing anything about it. However, almost all Protestant groups have always maintained many Christian colleges, and Jews who are so adverse as a rule to "religion in the schools" also have some notably good religious schools of their own. Our question here, of

[1] See the interesting remarks by Canon Bernard Iddings Bell in *Life*, 29 (Oct. 16, 1950), pp. 89–98:

"Most of the American people are religiously illiterate . . .

"Our schools were founded by those who considered religion of primary importance. Those who wrote into the Constitution that in our land there must never be an established church had no idea that anyone would construe this to ban religious instruction in schools, or to deny tax-support of schools conducted under religious auspices. There is no evidence whatever of intention on their part to make such prohibitions.

"Much of the blame for the change of mind must be placed on a shortsighted Protestantism," since it then asked: Which of these, traditional or modernist Protestantism, will be taught in our public schools?

course, is: What after all then, is a "Christian college"? We see the Protestant college—an indigenous
American institution—above all as a college where
teachers and students read and study the Bible and
where students become so adept in biblical texts that
they can throw citations and references back and
forth like a ball. Most students are Protestants, and
are either of one sect or are interdenominationally of
many sects.

Here the students work diligently on the Bible,
memorizing it and trying to understand its ideas in
their genesis and historical setting. What they come
to know in that way, they come to know, and this
knowledge is part of the total truth which they come
to possess. In nonbiblical matters also they reach much
truth, as much as and the same as is accessible in such
matters to anyone in any school. But what God says
to them in the Bible does not, on their view, afford
them truth, since (they hold) they merely believe
what God says and do not, on God's word, come to
know it as truth: it is matter of faith and not of
knowledge. On their view, a "Christian school" is a
school in which believers believe and knowers know;
and, though the same person is the believer and the
knower, there is no knowledge communication between the believer and the knower. Here the iron-
curtain effect tends to reach its ideal limits. Let us put
it in this way. Jones knows and Jones believes; and so
of Brown and Smith. The community of believers is

made up of exactly the same persons as the community of knowers. But I think it true to say that on some Protestant versions [1] the world of believing affects the world of knowing only in the sense that the believer's faith may inspire and motivate him to know.

According to the most famous historical designation, a university is a community of scholars. On the view we are now considering, a Christian college is a college in which Christian men and women believe and know, know and believe. They live as Christians; they know for secular ends and for higher than secular ends; but all knowing is in its nature secular.

A second view of "Christian school" follows consistently, as does the first, from a particular view of "Christian learning," as studied in earlier chapters. This second view is held by some Catholics, in fact by many vitally placed Catholics in this country. These good Catholics make almost the same rift between believing and knowing as do Protestants, and therefore they take almost the same view of "Christian school" as do Protestants. The difference between Protestants and these Catholics on the matter is that all Catholics hold that belief-knowledge is genuine knowledge: when I have God's word that X is so, I know it is so.

But as said earlier these Catholics for apologetic

[1] Cf. Frank Gaebelein, *Christian Education in a Democracy* (New York: Oxford University Press, 1951).

and propaganda purposes make a hiatus between belief-knowledges and all other knowledges: so much so that the two types of knowledge have nothing to do with each other; and the knower-believer is at pains, often by silence, to show that they have nothing to do with each other.

On this circumspect and influential view, then, what is a "Christian school"? The reply is consistent and logical. It is a school in which Christians, knowing in X way, know also in Y way, but in which the two ways of knowing have nothing to do with each other, and have no means of having anything to do with each other.

According to this view, which has the advantage of great simplicity, a "Christian scholar" is a Christian who is a scholar; or we may turn the terms around: a "Christian scholar" is a scholar who is a Christian. As we said, this view is both standard and influential. Let us see what it concretely means. According to its version of things the mathematician-philosopher Descartes, who was learned and was a Catholic, was automatically a Christian scholar, and a dozen or twenty Descartes thrown together in one school would automatically form a Catholic university. These good American Catholics who are good scholars are surprised to see what is thus implied in their theory of "Christian scholar," namely that a dozen Descartes would constitute the impossible hybrid, "Descartes Catholic University." But that would be the logical issue of their theory.

On the third view, matching the third view of "Christian learning," how is a "Christian school" to be understood? It is as logical and consistent as are the other views, since in each view "Christian school" and "Christian scholar" follow right through from the corresponding idea of "Christian learning." Here a "Christian school" is conceived as a school where Christian learning is possible and is being achieved. It is seen not merely as a school where people believe and know; nor merely as a school where people know a) Bible-wise on God's word, and b) secular-wise. It is seen as a school where knowing on God's word has something positive to do with some other learnings, and not simply as motivating, but in learnings as learnings.

In the preceding pages we have repeated this idea often enough to tire the least imaginative mind. Even so, it bears repetition, because it has now to be unearthed, having long ago been buried under the debris of apologetic and propaganda concerns, not to say wars, and long ago been lost, as we said, in the wake of formal essences trying to take the place of real existing things, and of good and needed piety put in the place of arts and sciences.

Because of these hurdles, it is going to be hard to sell the idea of the "Christian school" as a school in which "Christian learning" is ideally and really available. Not that the idea is a bad one, but that due to historical circumstances it is now remote from our actual theory and life.

The idea has some advantages, which we undertake to summarize. First, the idea is directly in line with the end and final cause assigned to schools by almost all at all times; that end, of course, is learning. Next, it sloughs at once the apologetic and propaganda idea of the end, and also the "save the faith, save the morals" idea of the end of schools. Thirdly, it is a positive idea, whereas the ideas just mentioned tend to be neutral and negative. Although, of course, school people get tired of study and teaching and the whole incubus of "learning," we need a positive idea: a neutral or negative idea finally lacks punch; the best it can do is to hold on, since it is not evidently going anywhere. In schools we want a positive and creative idea; we want the sense of worlds to take, to build, to create and re-create; that is, by the way, one reason why modern science, itself so positive and creative, inspires vast hopes and labors, and also why the knowledge of Orient and Occident, a knowledge demanded now by circumstances, could inspire fruitful labor. Schools need and deserve dynamic leads. A world that merely holds on is an old man's world— and one reason, a reason within a reason, why Monsignor Ellis, Archbishop Alter, and Father Weigel find Catholic schools failing in intellectual leadership, is that the Catholic school, as offered to youth in America, is not built on the idea of a creative intellectual end. Precisely in the line of the intellectual life, an institution of that kind lacks a hope, a dream, even a future, and in this regard, it is not quite fair to youth.

As we mentioned at the outset, the "Christian learning" idea was a chief dynamic of medieval learning; and to take a closer instance, for two generations learning in America was tied in not only with the idea of the endless creativity seemingly inherent in scientific method but with the now defunct, though once effective idea of progress, so much so that "progressivism" was pleased to align itself in name with that idea.

Dynamic, creative, positive, somewhere to go—all this is inherent in the ideas of learning and Christian learning, as it is in the souls of young people. This "Christian learning" idea was creative for some centuries, and now for two generations it has been the most creative idea for philosophers who are Catholic —as witness the works of Gilson, Maritain, von Hildebrand, Martin d'Arcy, Josef Pieper, and Yves Simon. We have reason to hold that, given a chance, the "Christian learning" idea has a permanent dynamic in it, not only for philosophy and not only for learning in general, but for the total social good.

We are speaking here of that idea in itself and also of that idea for the world of thought and action at large. So much is fundamental, and we stand by every word of it. The remarkable thing is that on our native soil and given our American Catholic record, the "Christian learning" idea has yet a fourth and very special recommendation. The record simply is that we have a whole school system begun and maintained by Catholics in America, but we are yet too close to it, too much a part of it, to see that it is a major achievement of American life, and possibly of all Occidental life, in the past century. It is a dedicated, consecrated thing, built on sacrifice: just when almost everything else has long been given to lush profit, here is something given through poverty and penury to the service of man and God.

Now for such an establishment and setup as the Catholic schools in America, a low aim and ideal just will not take and will not work. For these schools, an aim and ideal less than lofty will not make sense. It is ruled out from the start, and it would be impractical nonsense to think of it. These American Catholic schools have aimed high and continue to aim high— even, we have thought, in a sense too high: in their case, the best turning out to be an enemy of the good. We dare not ask them to come down from their wonderful heights in the name of any low aim and ideal.

The "Grand Old Purpose" of schools is learning. That, grand as it is, seen in an unmodified form, won't do for Catholic schools in America or anywhere else. We want learning, of course. Everybody wants it; nature herself wants it. But the Christian has a right to demand Christian learning and to settle for nothing less. At least so far as Catholic schools are concerned, we are not going to build them and maintain them for any lower learning-idea.

Here then in this "Christian learning" idea is a proper and direct-line end for schools, and at the same time it is an end sufficient to go on moving bishops and priests and laymen to build schools, and high enough to move nuns—nearly 100,000 of them —to go on giving their lives for schools. It kills three or four birds with one stone. It is the learning idea which is the proper idea; it is the Christian learning idea which is the only one sufficient and proper in the case of Christian schools, and it might help to get us over the hump of changing from a neutral and negative idea. Again from an improper though a high ideal, to a proper and grand positive, creative idea, it might at the same time prove sufficient to match or even to surpass the already great achievement of the American Catholic school system.

Let us repeat the point. The mere learning ideal, though a high one, might seem a little low and tame to sisters and others who are professionally geared to having one foot in heaven. They may think it too temporalistic, worldly, almost pagan. An ideal and aim at once proper, high, and inexhaustible is the idea of Christian learning. To scold sisters and others a bit and to help them begin to consider the quandary they are in, we ask them to read again the incisive words written for them and us (I am sure) two decades ago by George Bull, S.J., who said that Catholic educators are at times in their own way: "They call upon the ultimate objective of all Catholic life, the glory of God and the salvation of souls, and attempt to make this do duty as the immediate and specific object of education."

The end we affirm, namely learning and Christian learning at that, is truly the end in its own order which of course is the academic order. Yet in the total order, or in what Dr. von Hildebrand calls the cosmos of God, this end is truly a means. We are not talking about liberal education which in its nature, according to Aristotle and Newman and others, is an end. Everyone knows this as the point of which Newman made so much, and of which in our time Dr. Josef Pieper's great work on "Leisure" makes so much. Some values, though they are means radically and in the total order, are ends in their own order. Health is like this; play ordinarily is like this, and so is the nice happy activity of looking at a sunset or a river; and so is the nice happy activity of loving our friends. We just do love them and we ask no return or profit: the loving is an end quite sufficient to justify our act, though it is not the end of the universe.

Now knowing can very well be a means, and so can Christian knowledge: a means to a person's health or gain, to a community's health or gain, or again a step toward the common good of State or Church.

Learning or Christian learning can and does promote such ends (as Newman said of liberal learning), and in that relation learning is a means. This is mentioned here in order to emphasize the fact that Christian learning, in the sense in which we designate it in this book, has all the usual though magnificent advantages that learning in general has, namely that it is a lofty end worth going for even if it did not serve other ends. Yet it often does well serve them; and Christian learning, since, precisely as learning, it goes beyond ordinary learning, is even better, both as end and as means, than this great good.

Why this tall talk in its favor? Let us put it in the following way, now readily intelligible. If by revelation and also by grace, God enables us to know some things that otherwise we should scarcely know, or to know some things better than we would otherwise know them, or even to have a better chance to know them or a chance to know them better—well, so far, we have a belief-knowledge not generally available on other grounds. Then if this body of belief-knowledge can—and in other chapters we saw that it can—step up some knowledges not had primarily on this revealed ground, then, so far, we can have the learning which in this work is called "Christian learning." This learning is not only learning, it is learning with a difference, and we may justly say that it is learning which has a plus value.

If any such knowledge and learning are available,

their very availability will be an advantage for us in our learning and also in our doing. Schools making available this type of knowledge, and no doubt any other possible type, may be called "Christian schools," and scholars possessing this knowledge in any way and to any degree may be called "Christian" and "Catholic" scholars. It is exactly in this connection (as we have said) that Descartes, though surely a learned man and a savant, a fine unobtrusive stylist, and at least in his own eyes a faithful Catholic, may not be called a "Catholic" scholar. He was a believer and a remarkable knower, but it seems that he did not want to let his ordinary learning learn anything at the feet of his belief-knowledge.

Returning now to our third view of Christian learning and Christian school, what do we say is meant by a "Christian scholar"? He is not a Descartes. The Christian scholar is not merely a good Christian, or a good Catholic Christian either, who is a scholar; nor is he merely a scholar, however good a one, who is a Christian, however saintly.

This part of our problem is so important that we are glad to have the matter stated by two men whom we regard as Catholic scholars. Jacques Maritain writes:

Necessary as competence in his particular field may be, a Catholic intellectual is not a scientist or a teacher or an artist *plus* a Christian. His inner spiritual life superabounds *spontaneously* in the very *mode* of his activity, if this life is deep enough. No "proselytism" here, therefore. The very way in which he performs his ordinary tasks may convey some superior inspiration, without his being even aware of it.[1]

Or as Dr. von Hildebrand puts it:

A Catholic university would have no meaning if it were nothing but a collection of Catholic men of thought and science, while following the model of the modern university in its general atmosphere. It requires the conscious production of an atmosphere filled by Christ, an environment imbued with prayer; as an organism it must, in its structure and in the common life of its teachers among each other and with their students, be thoroughly Catholic. The students must breathe a Catholic air and Catholic spirit which will make them into anti-pedantic, humble, faithful, metaphysically courageous men of winged intelligence and learning, and therewith capable of truly adequate and objective knowledge. The demand for a Catholic university must therefore be pressed in the name of such adequate knowledge and met by any means only in the interest of Catholics.[2]

For our part, we want to make that statement more precise than Dr. von Hildebrand makes it. We want it even more modest and humble; and if perhaps "adequate" is too strong and daring a word, we want to say that we need Catholic schools on all levels for less

[1] In a letter to the author. Used with permission.
[2] Dr. von Hildebrand, *The New Tower of Babel*, p. 157.

inadequate knowledge. We have been saying over and over that the knowledge can thus be less inadequate because at least some of our ordinary knowledges are themselves enriched and fulfilled by their positive relation to the belief-knowledge possessed by man on God's word.

In the third view of "Catholic school," then, a simple and yet notable advantage that may be overlooked because this advantage is so close to us is that this view is really and perhaps pretty generally exemplified to some degree in American Catholic schools (we may in that case justly call them "Catholic schools" in our sense of the term). Because of belief-knowledges, some better understanding of poetry, though perhaps not achieved, is ideally possible, not only of Dante's and Milton's poetry but of Homer's. A better understanding of man is possible, I think, and is conceivably possessed, both by adults and by children, among Christians in general than among Communists or among pagans in general. That is the kind of thing that is hoped for on all levels, and is ideally possible, and may in fact be achieved at times, on this or that level.

It has its great and real perils, of course; but what theory of education, carried out, has not? The giant peril for this third view, the view that some natural knowings can learn something from belief-knowing, is that the teacher and student do at times in fact tend to let beliefs and belief-knowings take over where they should not take over; let them try to take the place of hard work and the mastery of ordinary materials. The danger on this side is a lapse into fideism and pietism; where work should be done, faith or mere piety is substituted for it. The danger on the other side, as we said, is secularism. Where our knowledges should be willing to be tutored by faith-knowledge, we turn into a community of scholars who divorce knowledge from knowledge.

There is not the slightest doubt that in the schools operated by Catholics in America, the fideist and pietist stance, the stance of "piety doing duty" for knowledge, is often a block to ordinary learning on the lower levels. There is no doubt that, on the higher levels, Catholics in both the Catholic and the non-Catholic colleges and universities are in constant danger of the secularist and positivist divorce.

Newman was circumspect, but we are not quite sure that he did not make the common divorce. He was aware of the "faith versus science" problem, and no doubt that is why he could write the following well-known lines according to which religion and science should be found in one and the same place and be exemplified in the same persons. He said:

I wish the intellect to range with the utmost freedom, and religion to enjoy an equal freedom; but what I am stipulating for is, that they should be found in one and the same place, and exemplified in the same persons. I want to destroy that diversity of centers, which puts everything into confusion by creating a contrariety of influences. I wish the same spots and the same individuals to be at once oracles of philosophy and shrines of devotion. It will not satisfy me, what satisfies so many, to have two independent systems, intellectual and religious, going at once side by side, by a sort of division of labour, and only accidentally brought together. It will not satisfy me, if religion is here, and science there, and young men converse with science all day, and lodge with religion in the evening. It is not touching the evil, to which these remarks are directed, if young men eat and drink and sleep in one place, and think in another: I want the same roof to contain both the intellectual and moral discipline.[1]

What Newman wants we all want: that the man who is scientific should also be religious and that scientific institutes should also be religious centers. He wants to end the divorce between the man of science and the man of religion and between the locale of science and the locale of religion, between the time of science or intellect and the time of religion or devotion. To this everybody at once agrees. What Newman seems to have missed, here and throughout his works, is the question of a divorce not less serious,

[1] John Henry Newman, "Intellect, the Instrument of Religious Training," in *Sermons Preached on Various Occasions*. This was the sermon Newman gave on the opening day "of our academical worship" in the Catholic University of Dublin of which he was the first rector.

that between ordinary knowledge, achieved say in philosophy and arts and social sciences, and the knowledge we have because of God's word; the old divorce between the intellect tutored by itself and men and things and the intellect tutored by God's word. Does the intellect tutored so well in one way learn anything, can it and should it learn anything, from the selfsame intellect tutored in the other way?

That seems to us the crucial question for "Catholic universities" and in general for "Catholic schools" and any conceivable "Catholic scholar" and "Catholic learning." In an earlier work [1] we kept saying that the two must come along integrally together and be made one world of learning: intellect as tutored by itself and things and intellect as tutored by God's word. A scholar with intellect thus integrally tutored and formed, and no matter what his field, is a Catholic scholar—nobody else is—and a school, no matter what its level, having administrators and the bulk of its professors with minds thus formed, is a Catholic school. In such a school, students are moving into learning and into Catholic learning, and their minds are becoming Catholic.

In short, our position was and it remains that Catholic learning has been created in the past, that it is being renewed and created now, that its creative wells

[1] Leo R. Ward, *Blueprint for a Catholic University* (St. Louis: B. Herder Co., 1949).

are inexhaustible, and that this learning makes Catholic schools and that nothing else can make them or indeed justify them.

Sometimes we hear popular statements about a "Catholic atmosphere" as necessary for forming Catholic minds and achieving Catholic learning, and statements about "climate" and "atmosphere" by scholars such as Maritain and von Hildebrand. All who know anything about forming man's intellect and his will must agree that climate, atmosphere, and environment are vital. For a school on any level, it is as decisive as anything could well be. Certainly in the order of practical learnings, which means all the arts and the intellectual virtue called "prudence," the atmosphere—Christian or pagan, Catholic or Communist— is decisive.

» 5 «

Dewey's Learning by Doing

THIS book is about the reality and value of Christian education. Up to this point we have exhausted all parties by saying in half a dozen contexts these things:

1) that Christian learning, quite conceivable in the first place and actual both historically and at present, is inexhaustibly possible and fecund;

2) that this Christian learning is a high-level end worthy of the dedication naturally expected of teachers and schools in a democracy and in a Christ-centered army of teachers;

3) that such an end, to put it momentarily in the double negative, may help to protect us against two identifiable cruxes: from not merely the best but the better remaining the enemy of the good; and from an unjustified gap between faith and knowledge: from what, to parallel Luther's famous injunction, is in

effect an injunction to secularize strongly and believe more strongly.

Now in order to speak again to learning and Christian learning as goods worthy of consecrated efforts, we want to proceed with a series of additional chapters. First, a defense of theoretic knowledge, which is knowledge of the necessary and unchanging—as if this knowledge needed defense: and here we will have occasion to praise Dewey and also to pommel him. Second, on Catholic Action and Catholic learning. Third, on the apostolate of Catholic learning now in America; i.e., on things to do. Fourth, on the vision of greatness natural to Catholic teachers and students.

In America as in many nations, people have a good and even an excellent temporal city; but knowing with St. Paul that we have a much better, an unfailing city in the heavens, we Christians tend at times to neglect the good temporal city and all that goes to making and keeping it good. Christopher Dawson says that the words, *Diem hominis non desideravi*, sum up the attitude of Christians for a thousand years: a case of the better and the best becoming the enemy of the good. As we have said of "merely natural" knowledge: some see this as not good enough and therefore as no good, a distraction.

That is not the only reason we sometimes do not like natural knowledge. Because of our laziness we don't take to it; just as other good things do, "merely natural" knowledge exacts a price: day after day, year after year at the courses, at our books, in the laboratory or the library. Two or more in *My* name working on problems, and persons working alone. This is tedious and hard on the activist temper. It is easier to contribute generous measures of piety and some whiffs of faith, and let it go at that.

Man confronted with God's word knows many things; i.e., he achieves a learning. Also man confronting "the world," confronting "nature" in himself and outside himself, comes to know a wealth of things, and achieves a learning. Then this natural learning can, as we saw, be fecundated and enriched by the God-to-man learning. For the present we want relatively to drop this God-to-man learning and stick to the nature-to-man learning. We want to break it down into its practical part and its theoretic part, which cover the whole. In that way, they form the classic division of knowledge into theoretic and practical. Each part will have a chapter given to it, emphasizing each type of learning as, itself, an immeasurable and inexhaustible natural good.

Let us state the good of learning in simpler words. In the business of sinking oil wells, drillers sometimes strike it rich; they strike what they call an "infinity well." This is a well which, when pumped for twenty-four hours, has the level of its oil exactly where it was at the start. Now each type of knowing, the theoretic and the practical, is a well, and much more truly than any oil well it is an infinity well.

In the theoretic field above all, men have been
pumping for centuries and bringing up truth, and
today we don't know what vast and intricate worlds
are yet to be known. Obviously our assertion holds
for science which, using hypothesis, experiment, and
exact measurement, can go on in a quasi-infinite series
of new and now unpredictable discoveries. We are
really overwhelmed with the riches of our knowledge,
and have not yet begun to put together into one synthetic whole what we know out of mathematics and
physics and out of all other disciplines, such as philosophy, history and theology and ordinary common
sense; some real promise of a beginning in this synthetic work is occasionally done by a few men who
know both science and philosophy, such as Whitehead and that most attractive of synthetic scientist-
philosophers, Émile Meyerson. Today still another
urgent problem of synthesis, and a vast one, is at our
door, the synthesis of Oriental knowings in many
fields with Occidental knowings in many fields.

Let us recede from the problem in those broad
terms, and let this chapter on theoretic knowings
stammer in the face of reality, and let the next chapter, on practical knowings, also stammer its piece.
Then for each chapter let us keep in mind how some
of our magnificent natural knowings are inexhaustibly enriched, precisely as natural knowings, by fe-
cundation by what we know on God's word.

Since the subject is knowledge and learning, the

talk is unlikely to be too big. The elephant unrolls his proboscis and picks up all loose things within range; many insects can reach far to catch what they want, and a monkey's paw is as handy as a rake. Through their senses, man and other animals rake up, pick up, catch things in another way. They take the thing in its outlines, Aristotle says, into themselves; they assimilate, not the thing, say a house, as its stands there; nevertheless, men and other animals take into themselves the sensible "form" of the house: and thus "know" this house with all its characteristics of matter, e.g., length and shape. The mind of man (we said earlier) goes much farther and knows what it is to be the thing in question, the thing "X," the thing "house" or the thing "man."

Besides knowing the nature and essence of X and man and house and good and evil and time and eternity, man, with the help of sense and intellect, knows things themselves; he knows reality and in that way he knows, not only essences, but existences. He is perpetually both intuiting and reasoning, and does the two at once. In intuition, his intellect "sees" something, all in one glance or *Blick*, as true; and his reasoning is full of intuition. Perhaps he reasons in "seeing" that two and two are four; he "sees" that one is one, and that one plus one is one plus one and may for convenience be called "two," and, having gone intuitively so far, he can "figure" out or reason to the conclusion that two plus two are four. Even from the first he "knew" that knowing is possible, that knowing is good, and he had the deepest "hunch" that he is made to know, and he "knew" all this not from reasoning and not from sense knowing, but from intellectual intuition (to "intuit" is one possible literal meaning of *intelligere:* to know intellectually is to "see" through things, intellect being possessed of a kind of divining quality). When we reason we go step by step, either from instances or from premisses, to conclusions, and though the whole process is one of reasoning, we simply "see" that we are to take the next step and that the conclusion follows, and this "seeing" is not a matter of reasoning, but is an act of intuition.

What good is there in any such reasoning or in any such seeing, or in a theory of either? John Dewey would certainly say and in many ways often did say that theoretic knowledge is no good. He repeatedly blasted it. He did this on the ground that only the practical is any good, or in another way he had of putting it, because only the practical is within our control; and he scolded people for having at an earlier time, as he said, practiced "the art of acceptance," and praised our era for beginning to feel control (as he said) passing into our hands.

If only the practical is any good, and if the theoretic is not the practical, then of course in this regard Dewey has said something basic. Before we go on to state the good that theoretic knowing is, we would

do well to review Dewey's view of man's coming to
know, part of which was expressed by him in his
charming book, *How We Think*.

In passing we must say that Dewey's theory of
education as "adjustment" to environment, is a wonderful statement of what education is. People are
sometimes at pains to belittle the theory by saying that
it holds above all for primitives. That is true; but the
theory also makes much sense as a description and re-
port of what education is. The question, of course,
is what education adjusts to; e.g., to primitivism, or
Communism, or Christianity. For instance, Christianity is always hoping "to bring up" its members, "to
educate" them in the ways of Christianity; and secularism to drill mankind in the ways of secularism, and
Communism—which is revolutionary secularism—in
the ways of Communism. What each wants is the adjustment of its members to its own pattern. So when
Dewey says that education is "adjustment," he has
said something that is not only true but perhaps too
true of education in fact. Whether education should
simply be adjustment or whether it should perpetually
transcend its parochial hide, is another question.

What then is Dewey's theory of how we come to
know? He says that knowing is by doing, and by
solving problems. That is the sum and size of it. He
says we come to know "hat" by trying on a hat or two
and by wearing a hat or two: there is nothing theoretic
about our coming to know "hat." So of our coming to

know "box": we make two or three boxes and use them, and then we know "box." On this theory, theoretic knowledge, if it may be called "knowledge," is irrelevant and no good: only the practical makes and uses things, and only it is relevant and good and true. Dewey says we are always faced with problems and are trying to solve them; that is the way we learn —by making a hat and wearing it, by making a box and using it or breaking it up. That is the only way we come to know. Learning is practical and problem-solving, or it is nonexistent. That at any rate is Dewey's theory, and we must now review his best-known illustration of it.

He takes the case of a traveler stopped at the cross-roads, not knowing which way to go. The traveler has to find out, and soon he is using every available resource. He looks this way and that, he squares himself with the help of a compass or the help of the sun or stars, he inquires, he tries out one road or the other. At last, he knows; and knowing is the result of inquiry and experiment: it gets man out of a practical fix.

That, on Dewey's theory, is how we think and how we come to know. There is nothing theoretic about it. If successful, thinking is the same as coming to know, and it is a practical process of putting one foot before the other and seeing what will happen, how things will work out. Thus the real test or criterion of knowledge—of "truth," if you like—is success, and the general theory is well called pragmatism: truth, like good, is a matter of consequences. Man is engaged in solving problems, and if we are to say that, more exactly, it is his intellect that solves problems, then we should say—so Dewey held—that intellect or mind is simply a tool, an instrument for solving problems. Hence the term "instrumentalism" which he used to describe his philosophy, at least in part; his philosophy, as he said, was instrumental, experimental, meliorist, pragmatic, and progressive.

Also two or more persons and even whole societies are always encountering problems, getting into jams —economic, domestic, educational, political, military, physical, and psychological—and a group will do well, if by learning its p's and q's, it can get out. Here again learning and coming to know are practical and are achieved in solving problems. Learning is by doing.

So much, just now, to sum up Dewey. Many difficulties remain which Dewey himself, a practical man, tended to miss or to gloss over. First are the difficulties raised by the fact that in trying to solve a practical problem we use much theoretic knowledge. The distinction between the two knowledges, as St. Thomas notes precisely, is this: when we know theoretically, we "know only," and when we know practically, we both know and either do something or make something. For example, when we know that one is one, or that coming to be requires a cause, we know simply, and we need not make a thing or do a thing: rather, we are next door to passive recipients of the fact or principle. Much of our knowledge in pure mathematics and in basic physics is like that: we know simply, and we accept knowledge with natural piety. So again of much knowledge in biology and of all our knowledge in anthropology, astronomy, metaphysics, and dogmatic theology. Through study in metaphysics and in physics we come to know nature, to "see" how things "hang together," and to achieve that knowledge we do not make nature over or necessarily reshape either nature or our own lives. It is good to know that there are so many, no more, no fewer, planets in the solar system, let the pragmatic, do-it and make-it chips fall where they may. That is an obvious point, but Dewey was weak on it.

Even when we are in the practical order up to our chins, as most people are much of the time, our practical knowing is dependent on theoretic knowing. I do not refer to the fact, known to everyone—and conceded by Dewey in his *Democracy and Education*—that practical discoveries in science, such as how to set off chain reactions, depend on and wait for basic theoretic scientific studies. Of course, all kinds of practical jams require "brain grease," and in getting out we learn something. That is perfectly true, and so far Dewey is right. But they also require theoretic knowledge. A bridge builder had better know the strength of materials, and a pilot trying to land his plane in a storm had better know which way is "up." But the builder finds and does not make the

strength of materials; he must, the most virulent pragmatists notwithstanding, accept most things as they
are; nor can the pilot of a plane reverse earth and
"sky." Dewey did not like natural laws that are simply
given and are imposed on us; and fetched up as he was
in the age of individualism, an age moving over into
the age of liberal socialism, he did not like to be dic-
tated to by fixed principles or anything "antecedent";
he wanted truth and good to lie only in consequences,
and he thought these to be simply within our control;
hence he was perpetually dominated by the idea of
"control" not only in his social philosophy but even
in his metaphysics and philosophy of nature. In his
view of things, we feel control "passing into our
hands." As Santayana remarked, Dewey suffered from
the dominance of the foreground, since it was "an
axiom with him that nothing but the immediate is
real"; his naturalism itself, said Santayana, is "half-
hearted and short-winded."

Dewey deprecated ultimates of any kind—principles, last ends, first causes, and his agnosticism was
based partly on this fear of the ultimate and partly on
what he thought the uselessness of anyone's possibly
proving God's existence. If we did prove God's existence, Dewey said, our goods and bads would remain
just where and what they now are.

In general, Dewey had a phobia in relation to the
theoretic. All the same, two and two remain four, and
principles, ends, natures, and essences, abhorred by

Dewey, are what they are antecedent to our knowing and doing. Besides having nature and reality
wished on us, we already "see" some unchanging
principles when we begin to control and at various
points to make important changes in things. For example, we gladly accept—we do not make—the principle that it is good to know, and the principle that
"good" is what goes with our being. That is why
poison is evil: it wipes out something of our being; or
in Aristotle's double negative, "surely that which is
destructive of the city cannot be the good of the city."
"To be is a good thing"—this is an antecedent, given
principle "seen" by all and given to all, to Dewey
along with the rest of us.

"Firsts," "lasts," and "natures"—that is the way
the world is, and though we have our difficulties in
finding out how and what the world is, and though our
practical doing and making help us in many matters
toward finding out how the world stands, still it is
what it is, and the antecedent, given being of the
world is the pivot and fulcrum round which any
successful doing of ours must revolve: in doing and
making we must square with the world, not the world
with us.

According to Dewey's theory, any student or other
learner would proceed as the scientist does. The student would set up a problem, and then go at it with
hypothesis and experiment, and at last come to success or failure, the "failure" itself being a "success"

because then one is presumed to know what is or is not a blind alley. One learns, one goes forward, one progresses, and goes with the world of modern progress. Hence the general theory called "progressivism."

This theory of "pragmatic, scientific progressivism" is so well expressed by William Gruen that we are happy to use his words:

Applied to education this philosophy treats learning as a productive, experimental process in which the student acquires ideas through his efforts to solve genuine problems with which he is confronted. The knowledge he gains is the product of his interaction with and within some empirical situation. Such learning is consequently much more than the passive acceptance of doctrine and technique. It is an active search. The student looks for the knowledge because he needs it for the resolution of his problem. In the classroom, as well as in the laboratory and the field, he learns by developing ideas in the course of inquiry. Being synonymous with action in a problematic situation, such learning is directed, selective, and critical. Ideas are learned in the very process of trying out ideas. In other words, you learn by doing: knowledge is gained in practice.[1]

In Dewey, Dr. Gruen and others, this position has far more than a grain of truth in it. We learn a great deal in trying to get out of tight places; and in the wide-open universe, much more than in getting a job or in

[1] William Gruen, "A Pragmatic Criticism of Community-centered Adult Education." *Adult Education*, Winter, 1955.

making ends meet, mankind is always in a tight place: man finds himself in a world where it is up to him to get squared with reality and to make his way around.

Let us now suggest how Dewey came to his theory of learning by doing, and his theory that theoretic knowledge, a knowledge of things outside man's control, is useless and does not count. Dewey's ideas on the practical were obvious, but from two elements in his own environment he got to overworking those ideas.

First, Dewey was overpowered by American practical experience. The American pioneer was taking a world, fighting Indians and killing them, making land and destroying land, raising houses, building railroads, building factories. The pioneer blood still runs strong in us, and it ran very deep in Dewey, and the pioneer is likely to conclude that learning is doing,—getting things done.

Secondly, Dewey's view of mind and learning is dominated by a phase of evolutionary theory. Dewey was at first crowded into an unnatural Hegelian corner for which everything was monistic, synthesized, and fixed; and then, under the influence of evolutionary theory, which he came to through James and Bergson, he swung completely to the other side where he came to declare that all is fluid and coming to be.[1]

[1] Dewey, born in 1859, seriously encountered evolutionary doctrine in the eighties; as late as 1891 his language and thought still bore vestigial marks of Hegel; by 1905, his philosophy was

As Dewey later said, to be is to be "in process, in change," and he summed up his own conversion in the phrase, "From Absolutism to Experimentalism." To us, by the way, he has always looked like a mind committed to monism: the world has to be all this or all that: if there is any fixedness, all is Hegelian absolutism; if there is any change, there is nothing fixed; and if action and doing are good and we know by them, the theoretic—supposing it to have any real status—is no good and we know nothing by it.

With this preface, let us return to Dewey's theory of mind and how we know. Under the influence of evolutionary theory, Dewey and others had an interesting theory of how man's mind originated and what it is. Evolution itself is the theory that some living species arise from other living species, and the Darwinian theory of how this occurs is variously stated as the "survival of the fittest," "the struggle for existence," "favorable variations," or simply "under the influence of the environment." The Darwinian turn of the theory is that in the evolutionary process some individual living things got caught in a trap; they could not get out and were doomed unless they acquired a favorable variation; to meet the plight they were in, some individuals did acquire this happy variation, they did survive, they mated with other individuals which in a like way had survived, and a new species accrued.

---

compounded of pragmatism, evolutionism, scientism, and progressivism and it remained a cross of all these.

Dewey's theory of what mind is and how it knows is a detail under that general Darwinian theory of evolutionary procedure. The assumption back of Dewey's theory is that some animal got into a tight place from which it could not get out unless it developed intellect to get it out; it developed intellect and got out, and here we are. On that theory, intellect is an *ad hoc* adaptation to environment; it is a problem-solving instrument, and Dewey's "instrumentalism" sums up everything. That is all that intellect is, and that is all it does; the child intellect or the primitive intellect, as indeed the adult intellect, does nothing but solve problems, and as knowing and doing, it is the prototype of intellect in sages and scientists. Knowing is doing, it is "manipulating"; as Bergson and others have said, man knows because he has hands.

We have insisted with Dewey that any child or man knows by doing, by trying things out, by inquiry, by getting out or trying to get out of fixes. In fact, man could know much more in that way than he does. He is always at one crossroads or another—locally, nationally, internationally; physically, politically—and he seems to be eternally at the crossroads of the universe.

Even so, man learns also by looking on, by seeing and contemplating, by accepting the universe, and by accommodation to beings and principles that are unchanging. Much of scientific learning, by students and also by scientists, consists in looking on, observing,

and doing nothing, though evidently much of it also
depends on manipulating and experimenting. Perhaps
more important, it all depends on prior, pre-experi-
mental and beyond-pragmatic principles, such principles as that learning is a good, and that learning is
possible, and of course on the principle formulated by
Aristotle and assumed by Dewey, the principle that
man naturally wants to know; and thus on the yet
more radical principles—not made by man's doing—
that man has a nature, and is by nature headed for an
end; or, in big words, the principle that man is teleo-
logically orientated. In short, for better or for worse,
man finds himself caught up in a world, himself a
thing of nature and with "a nature," a thing belonging
to the order of nature, i.e., the order found by man
and not made by man. To be wise at all, man accepts
this given order; and we conclude these pages on
Dewey's monist exaggeration and error by repeating
that Dewey, a rugged individualist-liberal and in some
ways time-conditioned, resented having to bow down
to the given world. Hence the title of a famous chapter of his, "The Art of Acceptance and the Art of
Control." A man of no compromise, Dewey was altogether for one and altogether against the other.

Dewey's is the activist, dynamist theory of knowing by doing, and of science taking the world; a man
swept along on the wings of that theory is likely to
remain unwarned by the fate of Daedalus and finally
run into what Maritain has called a "titanic demon-

ism." The theory is "rationalist" in the sense that it believes it is going to know all, and "pragmatist" in the sense that it sees knowing as exclusively a doing and manipulating.

Let us repeat as against such a theory that much learning is by contemplation. In seeing and hearing we learn much, and though the senses are active in learning, they too are at the very first step passive. This is a point made much of by Dr. Josef Pieper in his remarkable work on "Leisure." We look upon a rose, we "see" relations in mathematics or science or philosophy, and appreciate poetry or music; in each instance we come to know something we did not know, and have added to our own being and to the universe. Which is to say that contemplative learning is a learning, and is creative. It can be associated with a practical learning, but it need not be, and often is not.[1]

We are made to be—we want to survive; and we are made fully to be, which means that we are made for total development. We are creatures of nature, of course, and if by hypothesis we are totally creatures of nature, then nature has made us to be and fully to be; or if God had a hand in our coming to be what we are, still the same laws, demanding being and fullness of being, hold. If these laws are known

[1] Josef Pieper's *Leisure, the Basis of Culture* (tr. New York: Pantheon Books, 1952), is one of the most distinguished recent works in philosophy.

by us, they are theoretic truths; that is, we find them to be so, and here, in St. Thomas's words, we "know only." Evidently such laws, however necessary and however far out of our control, are important for the world of practical knowing. For example, in the world of medicine we do much making, unmaking, and remaking, but are perpetually presupposing that man naturally wants to be and fully to be. So too in the world of politics where we do much making and where practical knowledge is obvious; here also our practical knowing—unless perhaps on Communist theory—goes on the assumed principles that man naturally wants to be and fully to be.

So much for the basic dependence of practical knowing on theoretic knowing. For the unthinking man, the practical seems to stand by itself, but as soon as we give the matter a second thought, the practical seems naturally to demand the theoretic. In fact, people have for centuries known the necessity of this relationship, and we should not have to labor the point which was classically formulated in Margaret Fuller's words: "I guess I can accept the universe." The trouble is that we live in America, the nation where men have a lien on the pragmatic and where a pragmatic phenomenon such as Dewey should not surprise anyone. The nonpragamatist such as the early Dewey should be the real surprise.

Having learned well, almost too well, from Dewey and having a pioneer and pragmatist strain in us, we have to think twice before hoisting an antitheoretic flag. Let us be generous. Primary schools in America, including those taught by sisters, have learnt good things from Dewey. Though others such as Comenius, Rousseau, and Pestalozzi [1] had earlier taught this truth, American teachers of today have learnt largely from Dewey that little children even more than older ones learn by questioning, by handling things, and by doing—the children along with Aristotle, Dewey, Maritain, and others thus paying tribute to the empirical nature of the first steps in human knowledge. Yet it would be a mistake to suppose with Dewey or anyone else that even little children learn nothing by simply seeing and hearing, at movies, on radio, and television and in the wide world of people and things. Of course, they learn by their persistent questions, and of course they learn by doing. But to get acquainted with themselves and the world they use other ways, and some of them are more primordial.

Here we are cautioning people to give the theoretic its due. The caution might have to be on the other side of the scale in Oriental countries where, it appears, contemplative and mystical ways of knowing are ordinary and are taken for granted. With us in America, it will be necessary for some time to defend and promote the theoretic, and this in spite of the fact that science, in which we make great advances, de-

[1] See Laurence J. O'Connell, *Are Catholic Schools Progressive?* (St. Louis: B. Herder Book Co., 1946), pp. 22–27.

pends on the theoretic. It is true that Americans have begun to go for contemplation, a taste symbolized in the Thomas Merton cult, yet we will have to go on defending the good of contemplative life, and the good of a grasp of the unchanging, of a world to which our making and doing, like it as we will, have to remain tethered.

» 6 «

Catholic Action
and Catholic Learning

CHRISTOPHER DAWSON has suggested that we need
international elites of knowers. Mr. Dawson wants
these in the more human studies; as all of us know,
such elites exist and effectively operate in scientific
studies, since the ideal and as a rule the reality in
science, at least outside Communist-controlled areas,
is that discoveries are at once disseminated. Of course,
knowledge of any kind belongs to all, and knows no
racial, creedal, or national boundaries.

Now the truth value of science as the truth value
of theoretic learning in general is ideally for all, but
really it is only for those who can assimilate it; its
heuristic value, which means its value in helping to
make further discoveries, is limited to adepts in the
particular field of learning; but its use value is properly democratic and for all mankind. In these respects,

practical learnings are like science. The reason is that "art," which in its voluminous forms is one basic kind of practical learning, belongs to those who can enter into it, master it, and assimilate it in both its truth value and its beauty value. Now schools help young people to begin to live into that truth value and that beauty value, above all as these are expressed in the arts most accessible to us, such as literature, music, and acting, including the dance. But in this study we relatively bypass "art" as a practical learning.

The other basic form of practical learning has for centuries been put under headings for which our language has no exact word. Let us try for a moment to get at the thing and then fit a word or two to it. If a man does not know that two and two make four, he is quite an ignoramus; two and two do make four, and the realities back of the equation are the same whether he knows them or not. A man possessing such truth (reality grasped by the mind) is perfected, so far, and is said to have a "virtue," which is an excellence or development of the person. Also a man knowing how to make things in an art, in painting or cooking or words, is perfected and has a practical intellectual excellence and virtue: he is one up on the man who does not know how to work in that art. In any practical learning, some theoretic learning is presupposed; but theoretic and practical cannot be reduced to each other. In the practical, we do not merely know—e.g., that two and two make four; but we *know how*. We know how to make something. One general "know how" virtue is called "art," an inclusive word for the intellectual perfections of all who know how to make things.

Now for the other basic kind of practical intellectual virtue (for which we are seeking a name). This too is a "know how" virtue. It is the intellectual virtue of knowing how to live as a human person. Like "art" as a virtue, this "know how" also is enormously inclusive: knowing how to live as a person fans out into all of mankind's life of exercised freedom. How do we learn this "know how," if we do learn it at all?

Just now we must defer our reply. This "know how" is immense and at the same time delicate and intricate. All are to learn it. Hence it is more important than either science or art, and is far more democratic; not all are called to be and not all ever could be either scientists or artists, but all unless low-grade morons are to learn how to live as persons. All do learn it, though there is the question of whether various persons and various groups ever master it. If we don't learn to live as persons, we cannot live as persons which means that we cannot be good men, and yet all are called by nature to be good men. All who are good men have learnt this "know how" virtue and manage to express it in their action, even if many of them may be unable to find words to express the meaning of "good man" and "how to live as a person."

A man cannot have this intellectual virtue unless he has moral virtue, i.e., unless he lives well, and he cannot live well and have moral virtue unless he has this intellectual virtue. That is how closely the two are tied together, and that is how important this most democratic intellectual virtue is.

The name historically given to it is "prudence," a word now a little ambiguous and misleading. "Prudential" virtue is perhaps frightening—what would good people think if told they were full of the "prudential"? The best word for this intellectual virtue, a word used by Maritain and others, is "practical wisdom." Let us proceed with the thing so far described. We want to ask, especially, what the schools have to do with it, and how Catholic Action fits into the pattern of our coming to possess this "know how" virtue.

We must next ask what "Catholic Action" is. It is a technique which enables many persons to learn together and love together in the social order, and the adepts see that this complicated social thing cannot be precisely defined and also that the rough working idea of it must be kept fluid and not be allowed to congeal. But many beginners as well as adepts are willing to say that it may be summed up as an operative technique in the three words, "observe, judge, and act." In the ideal thus formulated, some persons or some couples of like needs, like social position, education, and income get together to see something, to study something; and this something is their own religious and social life; they size up what they are doing and what in the light of the Gospels they should be doing, and then they make a joint resolution to do it. For example, some couples in their twenties or thirties meet in some home; in the light of selected Gospel passages,[1] which they read to each other, they take a good look at their own life in some area such as work or recreation, they make a candid and public avowal and judgment on it, and they declare what they are going to do about it.

Is this—or any roughly similar technique called "Catholic Action"—a learning technique at all, or is it simply an "action" technique? It is obviously an action technique. But it is just as obviously a learning, since it begins with study and inquiry which are summed up in the word "observe," and often the inquiry is searching and sometimes is elaborate and may at times amount to a bit of exact research; e.g., what is the average income level of families in this corner of the parish, or which sorts of cuts of meat and which quality of vegetables do families on this income level tend to buy?

Let us see what our own situation is, let us mercilessly judge it in the light of the Gospels, let us bring

[1] The Christian Family Movement, which is the fastest developing and perhaps the most effective and promising Catholic Action form, commonly begins with a booklet, *For Happier Families, an Introduction to C.F.M.* (#2010, 100 W. Monroe, Chicago 3, Ill.).

it up to the Gospel level. These Catholic Action steps are steps in "prudential" virtue, and not only in living as we ought to live, but in learning how to live as we ought to live. Aristotle and St. Thomas would at once say that the whole thing now called Catholic Action falls, not primarily under moral virtue, but primarily under the intellectual virtue called "prudence" or "practical wisdom." Catholic Action people are trying to learn something quite relevant to their lives. Now, the main thing that all people are obliged by nature and God to learn as relevant to their lives is how to live as human beings. They could be trying to learn this, as most people historically have tried to learn it, in the light of nature only; or with people in Catholic Action they could be trying to learn it in the additional light of the Gospels. If they do learn it in the former way, then they have acquired the intellectual virtue of practical wisdom, and if they learn it in the latter way they have acquired Christian practical wisdom.

Our assumption is that learning to live as a Christian is something more than learning to live as a pagan. But each of them is primarily a learning. As Aristotle and St. Thomas insist, this learning—so far, like "art" —requires a doing, and a doing in line with "prudential" intellectual virtue; it also requires the practice of moral virtue, but it is not moral virtue.

In order to achieve this prudential "know how," we have first to learn at least in a rough usable way what a human being is, and what a defensible human society is: these are learnings in the theoretic order, since what man or society ideally and "by nature" is to be, is something to be discovered by us and is not made by our free action. But we have to learn not only what man is and that man is to be honored and respected—we have to learn not only the "what" and the "that," but how to respect man: the "how" of it. This latter learning is in the practical order where, as we said, man has two basic kinds of learning to achieve; viz., learning how to make things and learning how to live.

Great demands are always made on man in the order of practical "prudential" learning: always, at all times. But in the line of practical learning, new demands are now made on us. Long ago man reached the truth that "a man is a man for a' that" and perhaps in theory we Christians reached the towering truths that all are to be loved and that discrimination, practiced in all societies and perhaps most of all in our own, is a sin. But really to learn these truths by practicing them is more than a theoretic job; this practical learning, always an exacting and demanding task, is now an immense, nation-wide and world-wide assignment. Correct theory is not enough. We must learn in and by practice to love Negroes and make one world with them, to love Catholics, Protestants, Jews, and secularists and make one world with them, to love Chinese and Russians, and make one coexistent world with all non-Communists. Christ won't let us off, the light of the Gospels won't and can't let us off. We must learn, and it is evident, even in our own nation and in every community, that learning this as-if-new virtue of full-length Christian practical wisdom is going to take something out of our isolationist hides. Many of us nominal Christians do not want to learn this wisdom, and we give it bad qualifiers such as "nigger," "global," and a "pint of milk." But the fact is that nature and the Gospels are asking us to learn the virtue of knowing how to love all: and to learn this we must get into the habit of loving all.

So we have to say that "Catholic Action," in schools and out of schools, is, at least in most of its ambit, a practical intellectual enterprise, demanding action, and yet itself not essentially an action, but a learning.

Does Catholic Action as just delineated have any place in schools and colleges and universities? As a teacher I am obliged to try to understand about it, to teach about it, and in that way help and encourage others to learn about it. To understand *about* it, to teach and learn *about* it,—yes, but are we otherwise to have it and learn it in seats of learning? To learn about charity and to learn charity are, of course, far from the same thing; so, too, in regard to Catholic Action.

This question of Catholic Action as a learning raises the whole question of whether "prudence" can be taught. The usual way to put the question is simple: Can we teach people to be good? This is a question with which two of our most distinguished educators, Robert M. Hutchins and Mortimer Adler, have had trouble for many years, though the former has now begun to see the matter more clearly. Let us put the problem in the following way. We do not teach any moral virtues; we teach the truth about them, a large part of which truth is their beauty and glamor as well as their eternal rightness in the universe, and the horror and debacle of life without them, as seen in the major villains, racketeers, and debauchees of history and fiction. We teach about virtue, and by every sort of device and almost by chicanery we in the schools invite young people, almost all of them already good because well taught at home, to love and pursue good. Of course, children acquire moral virtue first of all and most of all at home, and Max Ascoli's assertion in *The Reporter* (Oct. 6, 1955) that President Eisenhower acquired his basic social habits at Abilene high school is naive.

Now for the question, famous even in Plato's *Meno* and Aristotle's *Ethics:* Can anyone teach moral virtue, and if so how does he do it? The fact is that people, born without any intellectual or moral virtues, come to have many of each of them. They acquire virtues, and they "learn" virtues at least in the sense that, not having virtues, they come to have them. So much is beyond doubt. We cannot "learn boys and girls" anything intellectual or moral: we teach, and they learn.

The way youths get virtues is not just the same for different types of virtue. They simply "see" with their minds that certain theoretic truths are true, and in some instances one simple exposure is enough for the child: he then has as a habit—an abiding perfection possessed by his soul—the truth that two and two make four. Other theoretic matters, if they are to be possessed, require more than one exposure; but in its nature no theoretic learning requires a doing. Now, all practical learning, whether in art or in practical wisdom, requires action; if art is to be acquired as an intellectual virtue, it requires some making and some repetitions of the making; e.g., in cookery, pottery, poetry, and surgery. It is the same in acquiring any moral virtue; this requires an action, and repetition of the action; a man does not become a just man by doing one just act, but by repeating just acts he acquires the moral virtue of being a just man.

But how about acquiring the intellectual virtue of practical wisdom? We must say with Aristotle and St. Thomas that if a man is an evil-doing man, a thoroughly bad man, he does not acquire it at all. To be a good man, he must know the end, a knowing which belongs to the theoretic order: man does not make the end of life to be what it is; and knowing the end, he must then also come to know the means to the end. Now knowing the means to the end is the same thing as knowing how to live as a person. But how does he come to know the means? Step by step, for one thing; and these steps, odd as it may seem, are acts of the moral virtues: if a man lives as a person in one act, he has taken one step toward knowing what it is to live as a person, and he can go on then step by step and learn to live as a person, and, tutored by nature and society and God, can learn as well as man can learn what it is to live as a person. But the man who knows how to live as a person has in fact acquired the "know how" intellectual virtue of practical wisdom. This very important virtue has then become as if natural to him; it is congenial to him; and we have good reason to say that this virtue of knowing how to live has thus, perhaps beyond any other virtue ever acquired by him, been learned by way of "congeniality" and "connaturality."

A child does go on, and he is tutored by nature and society and God. From nature, he has a start and orientation toward living as a person and toward being a good man, and thus toward learning what it is to live as a good man. From God, he has that given nature to go in that good direction and thus to learn how to do so. From society, he receives many helps; first of all, positive ones: he has good example all around him, at home and at school; he has example and prompting from saints and patriots and heroes; and on the negative side, he is helped by warnings and threats and penalties. As a Christian, he is boosted by grace as well as by nature; and is put in the way of doing good and thus of becoming good and also of understanding what it is to do good and to operate as a person. In fact, the Catholic schools at least hope that they are teaching Christian prudential virtue well on all levels, putting youths through the required paces, especially through the liturgical and sacramental life.

We shall have to insist on the point just now made, a point that is routine in Aristotle and Aquinas. It is this: By living in a certain way we come to understand in accordance with that way of living. If we live evilly, we come to rationalize that as if it were the way to live; and after a long while, we really don't know any better. Aristotle puts this basic point with frightening simplicity. He says that the man who has long lived evilly, does not any longer see the end; in Aristotle's words, to that man the end, which is the first principle in matters to be done, is not immediately evident; and of course the law of the end—namely, that the end is to be sought—must be kept on tap; but, says Aristotle, "the end is not immediately evident" to that evil-doing man. In our time we have plenty of confirmation of Aristotle's theory.

Take two instances. The first principle—"We are to seek the end"—can be otherwise stated as, "Good is to be done and evil avoided," and an immediate breakdown of this is that we are to respect and honor all men. But the totalitarian rulers, long habituated to doing evil and to riding roughshod over this principle, arrive at the stage where the principle, evident as it appears to those habituated to respecting it, is not immediately evident to those rulers. Another instance is that of the alcoholic. Innocent people imagine that this man can be appealed to by way of principles formulated in terms of respect for his family, his health, his religion, his job; but any of these, thrown into as firm a principle as one pleases, means nothing to him. Principles fundamental to human living are not evident to him.

The positive side is quite different and goes like this: Living as a person, respecting and honoring and loving persons, one comes to know what it is to live as a person. Aristotle throws the whole thing, positive and negative, into a cryptic formula which literally reads: As a man is, so he acts [what could be more evident?], and "such-like things seem good to him." Which, translated, means that the pattern of values that a man will go for is like himself and his actions: "as he is" and "as he acts"—this will dictate the things taken by him to be good; and such-like things he will approve and seek. That is what he knows in his "prudential" or "practical wisdom"; namely, things like himself. The formula tends to hold also for groups: a family, a church, a farmer group, a business or labor group: as any of these is, so it acts, and it tends eventually to take its own way of acting as the norm and standard of right action; and it will tend to suppose that everybody is out of step except our Jim.

Can we, to return to the old question again, do anything to teach a genuine practical wisdom—i.e., can we teach the intellectual virtue of prudence? We teach about it, we teach concerning it, we encourage and even urge young persons to live in a certain way, which (we say, in the name of nature and Christ) is the way to live. If possible, we lead them to water, but we cannot make them drink. But neither, for that matter, can we force them to acquire intellectual virtue; if matters are well put before them, we have reason from theory and experience to hope that all but the dullest will get them. Yet we know that some bright and capable youths will not get them. We cannot "learn a boy" geometry any more than we can "learn him" either practical wisdom or moral virtue. We help him to learn geometry, and are happy to help him to learn to practice charity and justice, and in that way help him to understand what it is to practice them, to live as a person and to be a good man. We are said then to have "taught" him geometry, and we may be said also to have "taught" him both moral virtue and that closely allied intellectual virtue called prudence. What cannot be too often repeated is that we have helped him to learn them. The teacher is like a doctor whose work is not to "make" the person well, but to help nature do what nature wants to do;

the teacher is like the midwife who does not give birth to the child, but helps nature to give birth to the child. The teacher helps nature to do what nature wants to do, and he helps learning to be born.

This is true of the formal teacher at school and of the less formal teacher at home, at work, at recreation, in the streets, at shows, in the army, and wherever people are who can learn. By many arts we are helping nature to do what in this regard nature wants to do. This is true of other institutions than the organized and the unorganized school; it is true also of the State, the economy, the Church, and the family.

Of course, in a society or a school that is religiously heterogeneous, it is difficult to help people to acquire and strengthen moral virtue and in that way to come to know better and better what it is to live as persons. Consider merely the schools, since they are the concern of this book. In a school that is religiously homogeneous, and is backed by communities of family life that is relatively homogeneous, the view of what virtue is, and of what some virtue such as charity is, has a chance of being a matter of common understanding and common word usages. The thing can be intellectually grasped, we can talk about it and point to it; and there is a good chance of some intelligent agreement and disagreement. In a religiously heterogeneous school, all this is more difficult, but we are not therefore exonerated from working to do what can be done.

After such a long preface on practical virtue, we return to Catholic Action. What we know as Catholic Action is everywhere now in American society, in the schools on all levels and out of and far beyond the schools. It is at least relatively a youth movement in the sense that by far the majority of its devotees and practitioners are in their 'teens or twenties, with a good little sprinkling of them in their thirties; and incidentally it is already the biggest and most significant youth movement we have ever had in America, with the exception of the 4-H. It is going to achieve much more, since to date it is only well started. But our interest in it here is quite special. We want to say two important things about it. We re-emphasize that it is a learning technique, a learning in the difficult line of the intellectual virtue historically called "prudence" and "practical wisdom." This learning of prudence goes on—as the learning of prudence always has gone on and always will go on—beyond schools as surely as in schools and far more voluminously than in schools. Little children of five or six toddling off to school already practice much moral virtue and thus already know, though inarticulately, what it is to be good and what it is to live as human beings. Then and afterwards they practice moral virtues at school and practice them possibly in ways they have not practiced them at home and at play; thus they may learn better and better what it is to be good and to live as human beings. In high school and college, they may come to some theoretic understanding of virtue and of how to be good; and we hope they may become more confirmed in being good.

The second point we are emphasizing is that throughout the body of our nation—in schools on all levels, and pervasively outside schools—Catholic Action people are learning the particular learning that is the most difficult and most necessary of all learnings; namely, the prudential intellectual virtue of how to live as human beings. We do not suggest that this is the only way those people are learning this virtue, or that they are the only ones learning it. What we say is that Catholic Action is a potent form of learning and relatively a new form, and that educational, social, and religious leaders, whatever their faiths, are obscurantists if they do not want to see its possibilities.

At least in the eyes of this friendly observer, "CA" is something that may go far in the next generation or two, and one feels that it could go far in the direction of a comprehensive good for the child and youth and thus for society as a whole. Catholics may want to exploit its potentialities, and all others to see what it is like, what it is doing, and whether some technique more or less like it might be feasible for many or even for all.

In the next chapter we want to take up learning, theoretical and practical, in terms dear to Catholic

Action people themselves, in terms of "the apostolate." Meantime, we ask Catholic Action people to
inquire—they are fond of inquiry—whether Catholic
Action is—and we repeat that Aristotle and St.
Thomas would say it is—primarily a learning in the
order of practical wisdom. As a result of their many
and diversified inquiries, these "CA" people want to be
forming Christian communities, and they are taking
St. Paul's action in forming communities as their
model, an action which itself was based on a body of
ideas and an understanding of the world. So this
chapter comes back to the idea with which it set out,
the idea of Christopher Dawson that we badly need
elites and teams of scholars, even international teams,
trying to understand man. Catholic Action people,
too, form elites, teams, cells—words they are fond of
—to try to understand in the most practical fields, to
understand and to do. We think they are in a position
to become the best students of Christian prudential
wisdom, and certainly they are appearing in bigger
numbers than students of this virtue have ever before
appeared. They are young and thriving and enthusi-
astic. We would like to see more of them, see them
appearing in more areas, and see them far better students. Of course, we mean in schools, and also out of
schools since this is where most of them operate.

Still, we cannot go with those who in effect (perhaps few hold it in theory) say that the chief business
of a school—whether kindergarten or university—

is to make people good, or with those who seem to hold that its business above all is to teach people how to be good. The teaching of habits of being good and habits of how to be good are functions of the whole society and par excellence of the home, and not chiefly of the school. People are to be good and to know how to be good, whether or not they ever have any formal schooling on any level; but in our society they know how to spell and read and they know sciences and history only because they have the added advantage of having gone to school. Of course we grant and are practically saying that goodness and the know-how of goodness are more important for us in the economy of God than any or all physical and philosophical sciences. That is not the question. The question is what the school finally and properly is for, and we are holding that its function is to help us to know, and especially to help us know the bases of things. If so, its function is above all with the theoretic, and, important as the practical and its know-how undoubtedly are, in the school they are subordinate to theory. Besides, they are subordinate to theory in the universe. As St. Thomas puts it:

"Perfect contemplation requires that the body be disencumbered, and to this effect are directed all the products of art that are necessary for life. Besides, it requires freedom from the disturbance caused by passions, a freedom reached by means of the moral virtues and prudence; it also requires freedom from external disturbance, and to this freedom the regulations of civil life are directed. So that if we consider the matter rightly we shall see that all human offices are brought into the service of those contemplating truth." [1]

[1] *Contra Gentiles*, iii, c. 37.

» 7 «

The Apostolate:
Things to Do

IMPORTANT negative things could be cited under the head of "apostolate." A person might emphasize things not now done, great desirable things. But these have been sufficiently said or implied and they will be implied again in this chapter. Just now we are going to try to sum up many of the positive things that can be done. Some of these are already being done by the American Catholic educational establishment, and in a single generation it can go on to do any or all of them. Many good things are beginning to be within reach. We shall put down a few of them under enumerated headings, as follows.

First. A moment ago we were saying that in our view and we think in the view of Aristotle and St. Thomas, Catholic Action is essentially a learning. We emphasized Catholic Action as a learning in the order of practical wisdom, since, as we see it, that is what it primarily is. We were saying that this Catholic Action type of learning occurs mostly outside of schools and outside of any formal academic setups. But now we want to emphasize two points. One is that Catholic Action leaders in America are—and quite rightly are —action-minded men. They are interested little if at all in theory, and thus action-dominated, and in the land—still, even today—of pioneer doers and pragmatists, they have tended to assume that Catholic Action has nothing to do with learning. On this point and only on it we scold these people, and we say that they and also our philosophers of education are missing a primary and essential meaning of Catholic Action. Our second point may be put pro tem. in the form of a question. Granting that Catholic Action is a learning, is it only and exclusively a practical learning? We believe that our best leaders of "CA" would say, "Yes, if it is a learning at all."

We are arguing on the contrary that "CA" may also, in schools and especially in colleges and universities, be orientated toward arts and sciences and toward pure speculative learning. Let us say that Catholic Action means that some few persons, lawyers or bakers or students or married couples, are getting together to give themselves the once-over, to see where before God they really stand and where they should stand, in short to make a group self-inquiry; and then, directed by God's compass, to see where they are to stand and what they are to do. Like on like, like with like, and for like: lawyers working for and with and really on lawyers, to see how to be Christian lawyers; and bakers on bakers, and students on students.

They are learning, as we have often said. Then they act. But why could not the thing to be done be a learning? As the result of the inquiry, do people have to do only quite practical things—to baby-sit on a community basis, to pay their debts, to make good bread, to dance well, and so on and so on? These operations are important, of course. The question is whether as a result of the inquiry some persons who have inquired as a group might see that their business and "action"as a group is to learn.

The answer is obvious. If group inquiry and group action are good for the goose they are good for the gander. If they are good for lawyers precisely as lawyers and for housewives precisely as housewives or for pre-Cana couples precisely as such, they are good for any whose present professional business is to learn.

Still, even in schools on all levels Americans are loathe to get down to business and to learn—to study and to master hard things such as spelling, arithmetic, reading, geography, history, physics, and theology. Possibly we need to be informed; but it does seem to us that American students getting together under the aegis of "YCS" [1] seldom if ever get down to business in the direction of "study, study, study; learn, learn, learn." Our position is that these generous minded Young Christian Students must above all learn to be good students and even to be superior students, pulling no punches and making no compromises. Perhaps their open-minded inquiry has failed to reveal a need to study and to learn. But we have our doubts. It seems manifest to us that their professional task is to study and to learn, just as the professional task of lawyers is to defend justice and that of soldiers to defend the nation. One could, we suppose, dig up cases to show that these admirable YCS people have sometimes made some such inquiry on some point, and have come out strong for "learning action" and, just then and there, have relatively bypassed "action action." But the cases of their doing so are rare and we believe insignificant. If significant inquiries of this sort are sooner or later made, there will be significant results, and we will be happy to learn about them.

It is going to be difficult to make these inquiries and to act on them. Why should it be difficult? For one thing, we are in America which seemingly is forever the land of practical people. Then too we are trying to educate all; and students come to college, to say nothing of grade school and high school, to get credits, certificates, degrees, and jobs. Schooling gives status,

[1] The "YCS" are the Young Christian Students, a sturdy and promising arm of Catholic Action.

and not learning. We want not learning, but practical results, good pay. This is true even in college and university, and indeed especially in them.

To inquire then where we stand and where as students we should stand in the sight of God and the light of the Gospel, would be a difficult thing to do. Really to see would be difficult. To see what is primarily and essentially the role of students is in our circumstances plenty difficult: to see that their primary, essential work as students is to be students. We would rather get by with saying, "Education is adjustment. It is maturity. It is getting the know-how of making a living. It is getting into the big money fast. It is making people good. It is training—training the whole man."

For these reasons, to make the honest inquiry won't always be easy. Still, we think it far from impossible. In every school with a dozen or more teachers, some believe in learning, and in any considerable body of students, say fifty or more, some readily take to learning and see the sense of taking to it. These are the teachers and these the students who, so far as learning goes, really and finally count. Like can act on like among real students as well as among housewives or lawyers. Let students precisely as students form communities of learners. For, after all, "community of learners"—of students or of teachers or of both—is the very idea of a college, school, or university in its most famous formulations coming to us from medieval university life. At times or places this idea has worn thin, but it has never worn out, and in any secular or Christian school it can be new and shiny today. It all depends on leadership. Happily, people have been finding Catholic Action leadership to be strong in matters of recreation and baby care and of worship and even of housing, in fact in many matters of community. Our question is whether it has to stop short of leadership in communities of the intellectual life. Could it be strong also in these communities?

We are assuming that students are in schools on all levels primarily to learn. We want them to learn without hitch or compromise. That (we assume) is their primary and proper business. They all have the same essential task—to study, and to learn. Catholic Action is exactly adapted to them, and they to it. They are all of nearly one age, all have like needs, all have the same occupation. The school therefore precisely as a body of learners should be a paradise for organizers of Catholic Action groups. In this case, the groups—"elites," "cells," "teams"—would get together to inquire, as "CA" groups do in any case; and as usual to inquire regarding the professional-occupational-vocational work of the members. If it is true that their work is to study and to learn, let them see whether in the sight of God and the light of Christ's teaching they are doing this work, and doing it well. A team of "CA" lawyers has to see whether its members are doing well their work as lawyers. A team of "CA" students has to see whether its members are doing their work as students. "CA" aims to give people a permanent "formation," so that they will be genuinely Christian lawyers or housewives. Could it not also give to students a "formation" so that they will be genuine students and genuine Christian students? We mean students, genuine and Christian, of history, arithmetic, theology, geography, and so on.

If professors really want to encourage Catholic students to study and learn, here is their chance, since in this way the students would be putting themselves on the spot as students. The whole thing is as if set up for the purpose. Students inquiring with students for the good of their total work as Christian students; professors, including priests and nuns and brothers, glad to stand by and encourage and abet. For the sake of the students' proper life; for study and learning, and for the development of persons in every art and every science; and for the common good of the nation and the Church.

That is one great obvious thing waiting to be done. To do it we merely have to shed the inhibition that the thing to be done, the "action" of Catholic Action, has in all cases to be something nonintellectual. The thing to be done, according to the inquiry and according to the best Catholic Action technique, is in line with the members' occupation and vocation which in one case may be to defend justice, but in this case is to study and learn. Don't then let these "CA" members by any dodges, no matter how sanctified these may be, fail to study and learn. If they do fail, they are no good as students, and to bless them then under the title of "Young Christian Students" is a kind of dishonesty.

All this should be obvious, but it is going to be difficult to grasp and assimilate. If "inquiry" is somehow doomed to be nonintellectual and action to be exclusively action-action, with study and learning deleted, then of course Catholic Action is no good to students precisely as students. What we are asserting is that it could be, and we are swearing it must be, an immense good to them.

Second. Such benefit should accrue not only to students, but again and quite naturally to professors. These good and harassed people always do form groups and teams of learners. We are saying that they have opportunities to improve on their present work in group formation for intellectual purposes. This is true in several senses since teaming up for intellectual ends can be in several directions, not all of them now fully exploited. For one thing, professors need interdepartmental intellectual life. Today, as Dr. Hutchins and others have so often noted, professors in one corner of physics can hardly converse with those in another corner of physics, let alone with those in history or theology. So it goes with professors of philosophy and those in English or American literature; they lack common ideas and a common language. This is a shame, it is a great loss for them and for the students working with them. We need departments, of course. But it is a good thing also to be breaking through departmental walls, and at lunches and at formal and informal discussion groups, even with set subjects and at set times, to be learning something of the wider world that belongs to a college or university. For twenty years the writer has been, strictly as occasion offered, bringing inter-departmental groups together, to discuss such topics as these:

What does Grant Wood mean?
Dewey's philosophy of religion
Graham Greene's novels
Whitehead's aims of education
Why the dearth of Catholic scholars?

The subjects begging to be considered by inter-departmental groups are legion—e.g., Lippmann; Oppenheimer; science and faith under the impact of the atom; the idea of a university; the idea of a Catholic university. The college and university world, whatever of lower levels, is running over with challenges sufficient to keep any faculty group busy the year round.

If all the professors in a group are Catholic, they may find it best to use a strictly Catholic Action technique. Often this is not so, and prudent modifications are in order. The group remains a Catholic-centered group whose business is learning. Of course this learning may be practical, for instance in the mastery of materials and tools in an art, but ordinarily the group will be engaged in theoretical studies and even when it is studying the practical it will remain aware of theoretic bases. Cardinal Suhard said these matters very well when, speaking of Catholic Action, he emphasized that the groups or "elites" would in his opinion be of workers above all, and then he went on to say that other occupational-vocational groups such as business men and scholars and scientists would also be formed. He then went on to speak directly to these Catholic Action groups of scholars whose research, he said, "must bear on pure truth and disinterested science." He said no apologetical interest should be allowed to get in the way: "You must seek only what is." [1]

Schools and scholars are glad to get the money of rich men, the blessings of churchmen and perhaps a nudge now and then from statesmen. But leadership and any growth and revivals of Christian or other learning must come primarily from scholars and superintendents and other officials in schools. The man who is to effect new life in American Christian education must of course be profoundly American and profoundly religious. It is too little for the man to be merely an American, merely a citizen and a voter,

[1] Emmanuel Suhard, *Growth or Decline? The Church Today.* Tr. by James A. Corbett (Chicago: Fides publishers), p. 82.

and too little for him to be a passable Christian. With religious leadership he must combine a passion for learning and for Christian learning and all this with a passion for America. Let's say he must be a Christian Dewey. And like Dewey he must be close to and work with the several levels, sympathize with the learner everywhere, with the fourth grade teacher as well as with the research man. A man from Europe or Africa or the Orient might well teach us the very thing necessary, but until he adopts us and we adopt him he is likely to fail to be an—and much less *the*—American Christian educational leader.

We are asking much of him—Christian all the way through, American all the way through, and as devoted to learning as a Socrates. Perhaps divine Providence will give us such a man.

Meantime we can do much. Dr. Hutchins hardly overstated things when he said that the chief function of the president of a university is to preside over a perpetual discussion of the ends and purposes of the university. Like the superintendent of any school he has to encourage freedom and joy in work. Department heads too have to go looking for scholars and to encourage scholars. In all this work, elites of professors and of officials and of both can be and are normally of immense importance. Each man is working alone, and each is working in various groups; that has always been the way of university life, and in general it should be the way of school life.

Groups should also be formed between school and school, at least on the high-school level and of course in and beyond college. Groups forming for the sake of learning—these will be the life of the school, since they will be the life of learning and of Christian learning. As examples we cite the practice of nuns at Notre Dame College in Cleveland who for some years have had an annual day or two of conferences for all nuns teaching in high school or college in that area: the result is clearly good for persons and schools; and the action of Mercy nuns in the Chicago area who are making a continuing re-examination of their schools from kindergarten through college.

Third. So much for these Catholic Action groups of students and again of scholars within and among Catholic schools. Almost as important as these groups are groups of professors from Catholic schools and professors from non-Catholic schools. Feeneyites would not approve these, but the question is whether we think we know it all, or are humble and willing to learn and to teach. On any level Catholic teachers need contact with their brethren from other schools; isolation and inbreeding are the worst things in the academic world. On the higher levels especially, we stand to profit by such contact. The conferences held at St. Louis University in 1956 were a model of the kind of thing we are for, a model to be varied to fit circumstances. Those three-day conferences were in philosophy and were planned so that on each day one central topic such as man's freedom was discussed. This was discussed from a Thomist point of view, but happily others than Thomists, others representing, e.g., American naturalism, were invited to speak their piece on what they understand by man's freedom and how they have come to take their point of view. The results, it seems to us, could only be beneficent and were in fact beneficent.

The point is that people in Catholic schools have something to teach, and they have much to learn. At least we hope they do not think they know everything. We hope their minds are not sealed up against the slightest breath of various and perhaps new approaches, new presentations of issues. Of course within a school, even a high school, there can be a considerable and a profitable exchange of views, and again between school and school within the Catholic ambit, or within a great religious order such as the Jesuits or the Franciscans. But we need and often we badly need to break out of the charmed circle, in order to learn where we ourselves stand, and at times perhaps merely to find out how ineffectively we have been seeing and expressing what may really be other people's point of view, or, for that matter, the truth of things.

What we are saying falls naturally within group learning and thus, in the very best sense, within college or university learning. For always we must go on saying that a college or a university, even a high

school, is a community of scholars; and now, with
easy and rapid communication, we can have a community of communities of scholars. Then too what
we are saying may well fall within something much
like Catholic Action technique: a group with common interests and common problems coming together
to see where it stands, what it really does, what it
should ideally be doing—and all this, at least for believers, in the sight of God—and then as a community, going ahead to do. Here the group would be not
young Christian students, but young or old Christian
professors. Our business is to learn, each one naturally
learning all by himself, whether alone in his cell or
in a more or less perpetual roundtable discussion. But
to suppose that we are not to learn with and for and
by others, and these at times of various philosophical
and theological complexions, is to retreat into a cave,
into a sort of loved obscurantism.

Fourth. The academic societies, sociological, historical, economic, philosophical, etc., are open to all
who qualify. Why do we run away from them? It
could only be because we feel we have nothing to
learn and nothing to teach. Few of us now frequent
them. Take one academic society of some distinction,
the American Philosophical Association. The division
of this stretching from Pittsburgh to Denver and
from north to south and including Canada, had just
one active Catholic member, just one Catholic par-
ticipating in its life and discussions for almost ten

years following the death (1938) of Father Virgil
Michel. That kind of isolationism seems unfair to
both Catholics and non-Catholics, since as philosophers Catholics presumably have something to teach
and to learn. We must add that when Catholics do
join associations, it is no good to sit it out on the
bank, watching the swimmers; the water at first may
seem cold, but even Catholic professors—let us say,
especially the nuns—must jump in and learn to swim.

Most successful in this line of mixing and learning
are the many small regional societies of philosophers,
common at least in the Midwest. The members come
to know and respect one another, and gradually to
grasp what men and women of other persuasions are
saying. Priests, nuns, and laymen learn to "get along
with" and to work with professors from state universities and from sectarian and nonsectarian colleges.
At least in terms of community, the results are considerable, and we think that in terms of learning they
can be notable. We may transfer to this and to many
concerns some words of Newman: Nothing could
be better for the Church than for priests and laymen
to get together and learn to understand each other
"and allow for each other."

The general word for the view that it is good to
work with other good people, in order to learn or to
do, is called "pluralism." Americans live in a "pluralist" society; America has many nationalities, many
religions, several concurrently operating economic

systems, and tax-supported and non-tax-supported schools. It is a difficult thing, of course, for those of diverse stripes, different economic systems, different religions and so on, to work together and form community. But believing in freedom and human rights, men in a pluralist society are called by nature and by circumstances to form community, and often they do it. Our present point is that schools need their own academic pluralism, their own working together for the common good of learning. People may say it would be fine to have an all-Catholic society and in that case automatically to have all-Catholic schools. That is not what we have, and a part of the realistic vocation of any group, such as Catholics or Catholic schools, is to learn to work with the total social body for the common good. Schools are no more exonerated from this duty than are individuals or families, Labor, business or churches. School people are to work together by studying and learning together, no one body of them too good or too wise to learn or too ignorant (we hope) to teach.

Professors from many schools are already working together, most of all in science and mathematics. For the common good of learning, professors must learn to work together in social sciences and legal studies and philosophical and theological studies. Think of the problems common to groups from many backgrounds and spanning several disciplines, problems such as science and man, natural law, measures of human value, the nature of history, the problem of war, the nature, status and possible limits of academic freedom, and the meaning and use of universal ideas. Professors have an inexhaustible job to do, and, to cite Pius XI slightly out of context, we need all men of good will always at work trying to do it. This is a task that nature and God as well as circumstances have set for us.

Fifth. Under "things to do," may we go back and pick up matters featured earlier? To bring a new look and new life to Christian learning in America, we were saying that we must shift gears. We must shift from the idea of saving good things to the idea of assimilating good things, from the idea of saving faith and morals to the idea of learning, which in itself is a dynamic and creative idea as various great moments in the history of Western learning have proved. The old neutral idea, the idea of holding on, has been strong and in its way creative: it gave us what we have in American Catholic education. If a sort of total effort can be directed now from the enterprise, already set up and going, to the enterprise of learning and Christian learning, we may expect even greater things. The thing itself is from a moral and religious viewpoint far from neutral, and it is too good to remain academically and intellectually neutral and defensive. We want it to be all that it has in it to be: assimilative, dynamic, and creative.

This shift has begun to occur. It is noticeable in the

larger colleges and universities, especially among lay
professors, a great many of them in a variety of fields
assuming that the natural business of the schools is to
study and discover and learn. But one notices the
shift also among more and more nuns in high schools;
many of these teachers now begin to refuse to let
piety, however good and essential this is, stand in the
way of technique and knowledge.

In fact, the most promising development in American Catholic schools in the 1950's is the Sister Formation movement. This was initiated by the sisters, and
is directed and promoted by them—and with great
success. They have found strong and creative as well
as prudent leadership among their own members.

They should do so, of course. This is a free country, famed for free enterprise, and the nun teachers
now number well above 90,000, and some say that the
nuns constitute one-tenth of America's total (nearly)
one million teachers. A few of the nuns, if they happen to be aware of it, are still shy of the question of a
total Christian learning: in their lives they want to be
Christian saints, but in their learning they are still
willing to be good secularists. But some nuns along
with some other professors in Catholic and non-
Catholic schools begin to grasp and to be dominated
by the idea of a total Christian learning, the idea of its
creative force and right and its inexhaustible fecundity.

Perhaps out of this amalgam of learners and schol-

ars in all types of schools will come a great leader
in American Catholic education, a soul with a unified,
comprehensive view, with a grasp of tradition and of
American tradition and of American Christian culture. Charlemagne asked Alcuin, who remains an intellectual force for all time in the Western world—
though Alcuin was not a deep or thorough scholar—
for a dozen Jeromes and Augustines, but Alcuin re-
plied that God had given only two. Alcuin himself
said that he hoped for a new Athens, this time a Christian one. For the present, we will be modest. We in
America would like in time to raise up at least a minor
Alcuin. Like the humble and unpretentious Alcuin,
we must be daring and experimental as well as meticu-
lous. Seismology and astrophysics as well as theology
must be meat and drink to us. When such a scholar
as Christopher Dawson comes to us with a great plan
for education in Christian culture, far from folding
up and pouting, "It can't be done," we will see what,
in the very line of Dawson's plan, is already being
done by a few professors and schools; again, what in
the Dawson plan is perhaps incomparably superior to
what for the most part we do now, and what we must
learn to do despite the cost and sacrifice in time and
labor.

Sixth. The Newman Clubs, long since active on almost every major non-Catholic campus, have been in
a way like the Catholic schools. There were set up to
save the faith and morals of students in what was con-

sidered an untoward climate, but unfortunately they have not at all generally gone beyond this important parish function to enter into the intellectual and Catholic intellectual life of students or of the college and university community. In a few places, notably at Minnesota and Illinois, they have done some intellectual work; but generally they do mainly a parish work.

Now, no doubt that parish function must continue to be performed on any Catholic or non-Catholic campus, as it must be performed in the military or wherever people live and work. But in order to begin to live the intellectual and the Catholic intellectual life, we must begin to live them. These lives are demanded on any campus. One by no means scolds the Newman chaplains who as a body are the most zealous priests in America. What one says is that if such a thing as a Catholic intellectual life is possible, this must be available to at least Catholic students wherever they are. Merely to look to the parish life of students and to leave them without an introduction to a creative and developing Catholic intellectual world is to leave them less than half-baked as educated Catholic men and women.

For all its good and all its sacrifices, the Newman setup is not yet nearly developed as it must eventually be. In the near future, more Catholic boys and girls will go to non-Catholic colleges and universities; also a bigger percentage of them will be going there.

Physical conditions will force this result—Catholic colleges and universities will not be enlarged fast enough to take care of the increasing Catholic population. The overworked chaplains will continue to run a race with catastrophe to try to save the faith and morals of those good young people. What we need and must develop, besides, are imaginative and creative intellectual leaders to give those youths the chance to develop—not merely to apologize and to hold on and hold out, but to sense and to live in and grow up in the fullness of Catholic learning.

For Catholic intellectuals in America, this will be a major undertaking, if we do undertake it, in the next generation or two. It will require the conversion of more and more Catholics who are intellectuals to a fully developing Catholic view of intellectual life, and the education of far more Catholics as intellectuals and as Catholic intellectuals. One excellent thing to do meantime is to have Catholic intellectual centers on the campus, centers that are completely intellectual and not at all parochial centers and that are completely Catholic intellectual centers. Such a center as St. Michael's at the University of Toronto would tend to answer the immediate need, only that we would vote for something less specialized than St. Michael's. Whether we got those centers or not, Catholic scholars and even priest scholars on every big campus would go far to answer the need; these would have to be scholars, say in anthropology or psychology or history or languages or literature, and they would have to be Catholic scholars; and if they were priests, their place of residence would have to be outside of parish houses and close to the heart of the campus. Some thoughtful people also say that an "academic ordinary" or bishop, parallel to the military ordinary, is a matter to be considered. Archbishop Cushing, e.g., has been immensely constructive in the Catholic intellectual life of Newman clubs in his area. Think what a full-time bishop-intellectual, a lesser Augustine, could do in this regard.

Since any university wants to promote all knowledge and the unity of all knowledge, every university "worthy of the name" (to use words Newman used in a like context) would want Catholic scholars, whether lay or cleric, on its faculty. In time our secular universities will have the vision and freedom to seek such scholars and to help develop them.

Seventh. We want to develop the sense of learning and respect for learning right up from the kindergarten. That goes without saying. But we want this respect for learning also outside the schools proper. We want it in our homes and in the whole Catholic society of America. Now American Catholics have the good fortune to be witnessing today the birth of extra-scholastic and extra-curricular learning on a serious organized basis, a type of learning that may in time take us a long way. Let us mention just two of the most promising developments of this sort. In Chicago, the Cardinal has said: "We must have Adult Education Centers where the laity can go in their leisure hours and study under expert masters the subjects which in our day must be known for fuller Catholic living and more effective participation in Catholic Action." As they see it at the five Chicago centers, one may say that the problem is for the adult layman to find himself, to come to himself, to begin to put together and understand the phantasmagoria of things and events ceaselessly passing before him. He would like to know how to add things up so that the sum would be the meaning of life and history, and of his own time and his own experience. In a word, he needs to mature, and these centers hope to give him the chance. Like and unlike that scheme is the "Collegium" established by priests and people in Shreveport, Louisiana. The ground was surveyed with great care before these Southern men and women ventured on it; then after two or three years of feeling things out, they launched their "Collegium." Groups of planners for any session meet in the pastor's office or wherever they choose; at first all interested persons in the area—say, seventy or more—met for sessions every two weeks in the winter to hear a panel of their own lay members thresh out some topic that all wanted to know more about. For example, the topic chosen for an early meeting was Lippmann's treatment of natural law in *The Public Philosophy;* the panelists were five lawyers from the community, none

of them educated at Catholic law schools, and not all
of them necessarily Catholic.

For our purpose here, most significant in this
Shreveport experiment are three points. First, in the
careful background work, it was found that in the
parish which was mainly concerned, over seventy
percent of the husbands and forty-five percent of the
wives were college people, and the question on the
one hand was, What good to these people is the ordinary, general and fluffy little ten-minute Sunday
sermon? Is it really fair to them, to priests and to the
community? The other question was, What does one
propose to do for and with this magnificent intellectual potential? Events show that these educated men
and women want more education, are serious in-
quirers, are of extraordinary good will, ready and able
to cooperate. The second point is that these people,
given a pastor who is aware of their world and the
wider world, can do much to educate each other; few
of them care to read whole books, but almost half of
them are willing to work with others in tearing ideas
out of serious books and in scrupulously preparing to
lead discussion on vital topics, and a big minority is
anxious to take intelligent part in this discussion. The
third point is that, though we grant the seventy and
forty-five percent in St. Joseph's parish, Shreveport,
to be exceptional, we are not living in the nineteenth
century: in the ordinary parish, it is time we ceased
to presume that everyone is uneducated and without

ideas or without a hunger for ideas. They have found in Shreveport that non-Catholics also have been glad to join the common effort; in fact, they made up over a third of the panelists in the first year.

The group from the area now runs to over a hundred persons, and the interest is so high and broad that in the second year the members broke into four groups, each working in a particular field: in sociopolitical theory; in science and religion; in education; and in medicine. In that way, each group is more specialized and can do concentrated work. In our opinion, something more or less like this educational venture, worked out in fifty or a hundred communities in America and kept from being swallowed up by any centralizing organization, could eventuate in one of the most important educational experiments in America. It might give us future generations of Catholics with an abiding interest in knowledge.

Eighth. "What to do" is the question of this chapter. The good things to be done, even the good things being done, are everywhere around us. The one we shall mention now is as necessary as any, and in fact the other good things are more or less hamstrung until this gets under way. We refer to a realignment in the attitudes and practices of the clergy. In America perhaps more than elsewhere, priests and bishops remain men of great influence, so that their attitudes toward learning and their practices in regard to it are of fundamental importance in the development of Amer-

ican Catholic intellectual life. What a shame then
that we should still hear even once in a while a low
or high clergyman, a disgruntled and skeptical man,
pronounce as if out of heaven that science is materialistic, that all great learning is in the past, and
that never again will there be great art.

Happily the positive and hopeful attitude and disciplined practice are more and more the order of the
day. One of our top-ranking archbishops earned an
advanced degree in social science at a state university,
and the late Archbishop Edwin O'Hara, one of the
notable creative workers in the American social order, was well disciplined in economic and social
science. Bishop Wright of Worcester speaks of
"Christians with presumably keener powers of in-
sight and understanding than the rest," and calls on
intellectuals "to find in Christ, the *Logos*, the Eternal Word made flesh to dwell among us, a divine
prototype of their special vocation and unique dignity." Cardinal Stritch promotes intellectual centers
and speaks and writes circumspectly on the place of
particular schools and of the whole Catholic educational system in American life. Earlier we mentioned Cardinal Suhard who called for Catholic
Action groups to be consecrated to pure theoretic
learning: "Your research must bear first on pure truth
and disinterested science. You must pursue truth for
itself without however ignoring its applications." Today, he said, "Christian intellectuals are everywhere

. . . trying particularly—and this 'positive' effort is a real novelty—to show that the problems facing contemporary consciences find their full answer in Catholicism."

The statements of these great bishops sound like a refrain of things which are repeatedly said by Pius XII in favor of scientific and general intellectual development. Of course, most famous of bishops to encourage and bless seats and men of learning was Pope Gregory IX who gave the Magna Carta, the democratic charter, to universities and who in the years when Thomas Aquinas was a little boy was christening the university as "mother of sciences, city of letters," a city where learned men "shine as a candle on the candlestick."

To begin to bring Catholic learning in America toward fruition many steps will be helpful. One of the biggest and most necessary will be for seminarians and their superiors, and novices and their masters in all orders and congregations, to learn to work actively to respect sciences and arts. They now learn to respect God, and the Word, and we hope they also learn to see as sacred every nation and every man and also nature herself. Besides, they must learn to stand in awe before man's attempt to transcribe nature and God and man, before man's attempt to stammer Jeremiah's "Ah, ah, ah, Lord God" in the face of these realities. It would be a great thing for their own lives and for the Church in America if seminarians should begin to find life and joy in learning. We grant that as priests they will be engaged in the active apostolate. But it would be a grand thing for all concerned if—to take one matter—when they preached they knew the original text and the context of any scriptural passages they used. Think what it would mean to them and to the people, and to the dignity of learning, if priests were to go to the original words of St. Paul, St. John, and Isaiah, and if they knew why this or that "new" translation is made as it is made. Again, to see the paschal sacrifice in the light of the best historical studies (pastors could hardly go to sources) would be a tremendous thing for both our priests and our people. Also seminarians must be groomed and disciplined to use factual empirical studies whenever these are available, so that people won't be forever subjected to preachers' unsupported and unverified broadsides.

With a little shift in gears, a little change in attitudes and practices, such things can begin to be, and after a century the record would tell a different story. It would not matter whence the shift came—from a new divine inspiration in Catholic or secular universities, from the bishops' blessing, from international shocks, from liturgical or action interests. It would be excellent, too, if more and more priests became adept in American history or American literature, or in our deepest modern aspirations such as those for freedom and the love of all men, or in great

Americans such as Lincoln, Jefferson, and Gibbons. A few months after becoming pope, Pius XII wrote a letter [1] to America asking American priests to learn to study. First he lamented evils such as divorce and its consequences, and then said these words which should become mottoes for American Catholics, clergy and lay, for schools and parishes and even for homes:

A very efficacious means for driving out such grave evils is that individual Catholics receive a thorough training in the divine truths and that the people be shown clearly the road which leads to salvation.

Therefore, we exhort priests to provide that their own knowledge of things divine and human be wide and deep; that they be not content with the intellectual knowledge acquired in youth; that they examine with careful scrutiny the Law of the Lord, whose oracles are purer than silver; that they continually relish and enjoy the chaste charms of Sacred Scripture; that with the passing of the years they study more deeply the history of the Church, its dogmas, its sacraments, its laws, its scriptions, its liturgy, its language, so that they may advance in grace, in culture and wisdom.

Let them cultivate also the study of letters and of the profane sciences, especially those which are more closely connected with religion, in order that they may be able to impart with clarity and eloquence the teaching of grace and salvation which is capable of bending even

[1] Pius XII, "The Crown of Joy" (*Sertum laetitiae*), Nov. 1, 1939; a letter to the U.S.A.

learned intellects to the light burden and yoke of the Gospel of Christ.

Fortunate the Church, indeed, if thus it will lay its "foundations with sapphires" (cf. Isaias, 54, 11). The needs of our times then require that the laity, too, and especially those who collaborate with the hierarchy of the Church, procure for themselves a treasure of religious knowledge, not a poor and meager knowledge, but one that will have solidity and richness through the medium of libraries, discussions, and study clubs; in this way they will derive great benefit for themselves and at the same time be able to instruct the ignorant, confute stubborn adversaries and be of assistance to good friends. . . .

Because of our constant desire that scientific progress in all its branches be ever more universally affirmed . . .

Only Heaven itself—or perhaps Pius XII—could enumerate all the studies or even the areas in which seminarians and priests might well be interested and in which they would be happy to see the truth. Of course it is up to the particular man to create times and places of "leisure," in Dr. Pieper's sense of the word, to read, digest, meditate, contemplate, and to confer with priests and laymen who practice these arts. Given this impetus and this kind of practice, and given the often generous and liberal educational background of the American priest, we could scarcely set limits to what priests can do to promote and inspire and create learning in America. Laymen and non-Catholics will welcome priests in these intellectual roles, for the good of the whole thing of which we write in this chapter and this book, namely a growing up together in wisdom and in Christian wisdom.

» 8 «

A Vision of Greatness

TEACHERS have to aim high, and to hold a vision of greatness before the minds and hearts of pupils, a vision of greatness in the knowledge and appreciation of every human and divine thing. We want to emphasize the need of presenting that vision in the materials of education and the realities back of the materials, and in this regard we think the Catholic educator has an advantage and a golden opportunity. In learning and knowledge proper, say in poetry and science and history, and again in Christian learning wherever this as we have conceived it has application, the half-hearted, little-souled, picayune teacher would not make sense. We say with Whitehead and all genuine educators that the child must learn precision habits of thought, and in some parts of some sciences he must learn to use precision instruments. That goes without saying. But we are no good as teachers if we do not let the child, and the young man and woman, too, in their learning discover and enjoy (or suffer) the immensity of things, the endless complexity of things; in their learning, let them see the heroic and also the miserable character of man and of particular men, saints and villains, and the nearness of God's love: as the Irish say, "God's help is nearer than the door." The child, made to know all truth and to love all good, already has by nature a running start toward greatness: he seems to sense, as if by a previous incarnation, that his mind and will are quasi infinities, capable of and made for all being; in St. Augustine's words, *Capax Dei,* and St. Thomas's words, *Capax universi.*

As prelude to a vision of greatness, we cite the words of three distinguished English educators. Perhaps the most famous of all English educators, Alcuin alone excepted, was Thomas Arnold, headmaster of Rugby over a century ago. Arnold said that everything associated with a school should give the students a "lift" and a sense of greatness:

There is, or there ought to be, something very ennobling in being connected with an establishment at once ancient and magnificent, where all about us, and all the associations belonging to the objects around us, should be great, splendid, and elevating. What an individual ought and often does derive from the feeling that he is born of an old and illustrious race, from being familiar from his childhood with the walls and trees which speak of the past no less than of the present, and make both full of images of greatness; this, in an inferior degree, belongs to every member of an ancient and celebrated place of education.[1]

Speaking of what good an education in Latin literature is to modern man, Whitehead said its function is

... its expression of greatness. ... The understanding of Rome leads back to that Mediterranean civilization of which Rome was the last phase. ... The merit of this study in the education of youth is its concreteness, its inspiration to action, and the uniform greatness of persons, in their characters and their staging. Their aims were great, their virtues were great, and their vices were great. They had the saving merit of sinning with cart-ropes. Moral education is impossible apart from the habitual vision of greatness. If we are not great, it does not matter what we do or what is the issue. Now the sense of greatness is an immediate intuition and not the conclusion of an argument. It is permissible for youth in the agonies of religious conversion to entertain the feeling of being a worm and no man, so long as there remains the conviction of greatness sufficiently to justify the eternal wrath of God. The sense of greatness is the groundwork of morals. We are at the threshold of a democratic age, and it remains to be determined whether the equality of man is to be realized on a high level or a low level. There was never a time in which it was

[1] Arthur P. Stanley, *The Life and Correspondence of Thomas Arnold*. Sixth edition (London: 1846), p. 86.

more essential to hold before the young the vision of Rome: in itself a great drama, and with issues greater than itself.[1]

The third educator says the same. After saying that an education must not try to do everything, and that it "prospers by economy, by exclusion," Sir Richard Livingstone says [2] that the first principle is that certain subjects, not more than two, "must be studied so thoroughly that the pupil gets some idea of what knowledge is. That lesson cannot be learnt by studying a large number of things; it demands time and concentration. The second principle is that these subjects should bring the pupil face to face with something great. Nothing—not all the knowledge in the world—educates like a vision of greatness, and nothing can take its place. Now the old classical education satisfied these two principles. Those whom it suited learnt two subjects pretty thoroughly, and thereby got a glimpse of what knowledge is and of the price which it exacts: and they met greatness in two great literatures."

In these pages we wield no shillelagh for or against the "old classical education," but we take our stand for the principle of being educated in, and we may say by and for, a sense of greatness, a sense that must

[1] Alfred North Whitehead, *The Aims of Education* (A Mentor book: 3rd printing, 1952), p. 77.
[2] Sir Richard Livingstone, *Some Tasks for Education* (New York: Oxford University Press, 1946), pp. 17–18.

affect and dominate the teacher and administrator as well as the pupil. At any rate, nothing pusillanimous will do for the child—the child of man, or the child of the Christian, or the American. Youth thrives on the daring, the heroic, even on the call to martyrdom, as witness the place of college students in fights for freedom, and as witness the appeal of Maryknoll and Grailville, each of which has a world-wide view and asks youth to be completely magnanimous in giving. Youth likes the kind of "big talk" David Riesman uses to conclude an essay: "Make no little plans; they have no magic to stir men's blood and probably themselves will not be realized. Make big plans: aim high in hope and work, remembering that a noble, logical diagram, once recorded, will never die."

We must be particular, exact and exacting. But we must aim at vastness, at great inspiring views of man and society, of heroes and nations, of nature as grand and beautiful and awe-inspiring, of God as lord of nature and of all free men. It is easy enough, of course, to sense the "big" in mission work—and we must say that the Catholic Students Mission Crusade appeals to greatness justifiably and well; but in our ordinary, humdrum schoolwork, how is that to be done? The rest of this chapter says in effect that, given our materials, how can we fail to do it?

The summary of great things being seen by teacher and student is God, nature, and man. Let us take the last first. Through studies, especially in literature and history, we want to let the child see man in all his desegregated greatness. We want to give the child a chance to grow into a profound and, if possible in the case—granting his inherent and environmental limitations—an overwhelming belief in man. If possible, we would like him to come to believe in man as simply and mightily as Abraham Lincoln believed in man; and we school people keep inviting him, in story and poetry, in history, in geography, in science, in psychology, through books and pictures and drama and talks and discussions—we keep inviting the child to a great belief in man, in man as free, as enslaved, as struggling for freedom, as resourceful, as a person like God, and as invincible as the record shows man to be. As a lover of man, as the conqueror of worlds, as penetrating the heart and being of things, as seeing invisible relations, as dissecting the impenetrable, as saint, as falling and rising again. Poor man, rich man, terrible, intolerable man, wise and ignorant, dying hundreds of times and yet he lives. That great being is what we want to allow the child to know.

Man is perhaps best seen through studies in history, literature, and art, though psychology is welcome to help fill in the picture; and anthropology, whether something really distinct from history, may tell its story and help along the whole. One advantage of the "man" story, the vision of greatness in man, is that it need not, at least for little children and up to half way through high school, draw close distinctions between nature and grace. It is "man" whom the child is seeing, and it is an afterthought of the advanced specialist that draws fine distinctions.

Let the child alone. Let that child be. Let him look on man, first as a sort of mystic, unreal creature almost like men in fairy tales; then on man as living so wondrously in poetry; then on man as seen in the story of great civilizations and lastly in the great cultures, whether civilized or not. At this point we are not saying how the child is to come to see man, how he comes to know man and civilizations and cultures; we are simply mentioning them as objects of giant stature for the child to look at; and while it is true that civilizations and cultures go up and down as if on a lever, the important thing for the child's growth is to see them, whatever they are and whatever they do. The drama of "man" is much too good for the child to miss.

Take just one passage in Homer inviting us to see beauty and truth and terror in man. The child, delighted to read and contemplate the Homeric creations in general, will be especially delighted to see man and the Greeks and Achilles, and incidentally Homer himself, as these are concretely and beautifully expressed on the shield of Achilles (*Iliad*, book 18). On the shield a heavenly blacksmith-artist named Hephaestus wrought earth and heaven, and the sea, and the sun, and the full moon; and two cities of men, beautiful—and we may say, terrible—to behold. In one of them were a marriage and feasting, the bridal procession going through the city by the light of torches, and boys dancing to the music of flutes and lyres. "Downtown" a quarrel took place between two men about the penalty to be paid for a man who had been killed; the judges sitting on polished stone seats in a sacred circle. The other city was surrounded by two armies, ready to plunder or destroy; but the men of the city, refusing surrender, were in ambush, and the women were guarding the city wall; a battle broke out along the river banks; spears flew through the air; the demons of war moved among the men, and the spirit of death, all bloodstained, dragged the dead and wounded through the melee. Not yet content, Hephaestus did a lovely rural scene: ploughmen serving wine and reapers binding their sheaths, the king in joyful silence surveying the whole; a vine-yard, and shepherds and cattle and dogs; young men and maidens dancing, and a divine minstrel singing to his lyre.

Little children from the fifth to the eighth grade would simply follow the action in this picture and throughout Homer and love it because it has simplicity and grandeur; and bigger children would begin to sense the beauty and truth and terror in the action along with the simplicity and grandeur. For the most part, till at least into college they should be let alone to enjoy Homeric and other stories, and neither children nor stories should be torn apart or dissected by variant readings and philological and casuistic details. The wholeness of the thing—in Job or Homer, Vergil or Shakespeare—will come to children, if not as they first read, then surely as they re-read in after years and as the stories return in memory to them, since of course they should be visualizing and memorizing,—the wholeness will come over them, and the harmony of man and nature, and of heaven and earth, and the beauty. Children cannot yet grasp theory, or the relevance of exegetics, or what philosophical and theological studies could possibly mean. But they grasp wholeness, meaning, joy, fear, the unity and majesty of great literature, and great moments in history.

In inviting and encouraging children to read great things and to see great things in movies and on television, the important thing is to encourage freedom and joy. Children don't automatically know and select good things, and if teachers have any function at all in relation to children it surely includes the selection of things excellent to read and to see. It is inhuman, indecent, and degrading—and if democratic, then democracy is, so far, an evil thing—to have children's senses and minds and affections exposed, day by day and hour by hour, in movies and in television, to trash that seemingly "pays off." There is a difference between "good" and "evil" in art as well as in things and in human acts, and a main function of the educator is to help children grow up learning to enjoy the good and to hate evil. So Plato wisely said, and on this point Aristotle was happy to agree with him. The child cannot yet judge—but he can learn to judge— good and evil in action and in art, and to judge them for himself: this effect is the central and major value of a liberal education, and even in schooling the whole people and in encouraging studies in science, we have to give everyone the chance to move, at least some little way, into the main good of liberal education— which, to repeat, is to be able to judge the most human things.

Here we have been engaged in saying that the child should be introduced to a vision of man's greatness, Athenian greatness, Chinese greatness, American greatness, in general to human greatness. All the miserly minds in the world, taken in their lump sum, should not be allowed to cheat the child out of this vision of man's greatness.

Next, about God's greatness. This should be an easy lesson, something absorbed as the air is breathed, and though exactly what the students are learning about God and how they are learning it depends on the age and maturity-immaturity of the students, the important thing is that they come, in one way or another but as soon as feasible, to stand in awe before God. In this enterprise, Moses helps, Job and David help, Jesus Himself is invaluable. St. John the Evangelist helps, Dante helps, Milton helps, and the liturgical life, effected by families and schools and parishes, is indispensable. The little child can learn the Our Father and the Glory be to the Father. Once I visited the home of a Mennonite family of Swiss origin in a community of like origin, and as blessing at dinner the father and mother and son and daughter sang the Glory be to the Father in four parts. Children could learn not only to "say" but to sing prayers at home and in school and church and community.

To illustrate learning "about" the majesty of God, and even coming to grasp that majesty, some words spoken by Job on a famous occasion will do. Job had lost everything, and his neighbors, peasant farmers like himself, came to console him. These good neighbors improvised magnificent songs about the greatness of God. Then Job (chapter 26) outdoing them all, answered and said:

Behold the giants groan under the waters,
and they that dwell with them.

Hell is naked before Him,
and there is no covering for destruction.

He stretched out the north over the empty space,
and hangeth the earth upon nothing.

He bindeth up the waters in his clouds,
so that they break not out and fall down together.

He withholdeth the face of his throne
and spreadeth his cloud over it.

He hath set bounds about the waters,
till light and darkness come to an end.

The pillars of heaven tremble
and dread at his beck.

By his power the seas are suddenly gathered together,
and his wisdom has struck the proud one.

His spirit hath adorned the heavens,
and his obstetric hand brought forth the winding ser-
pent.

Lo, these things are said in part of his ways:
and seeing we have heard scarce a little drop of his word,
who shall be able to behold the thunder of his greatness?

Let little children come to hear and sing such great
things; let them memorize and sing a few psalms such
as the ninety-fifth: "Sing ye to the Lord a new song."

When it is a question of knowing nature and won-
dering at its greatness, we are again naturally invited,
at any time and surely in modern times, to catch our
breath. "Nature," the world around us and within us,
and ourselves as part of that over-all "nature"—all this
is of course taken for granted by the child. It is just
"there," and as the child sees things, it was always there
and always operating as it now operates; which means
that, except that he easily knows God, the child is as
if a natural devotee of naturalism, in the present sense
of "naturalism" in American philosophy. The child

wants to see and contemplate things of nature. That is all there is to it. We adults are the ones who think that our own knowledge of nature and our own minor bit of control over nature is "something," and in the modern Occident we are likely to be bumptious and arrogant over our bit of knowledge and control. That men should sail up five or six miles into the sky, or crawl on the bottom of the sea, or find out how to blow up everything with bombs, is as nothing to the child. He takes such things for granted, because he never saw a society that could not do them. For his part, a dog or a pony is something greater, or a baby brother of any color to play with. But here again he is meeting nature —and in some of its vivid and moving forms.

As he advances in years and wisdom, we can begin to introduce him, through chats and books and pictures and travel, to the sea and mountains and even to foreign peoples and their customs, still so strange to us adults; and we must say in passing that some of the better televised action-pictures of life abroad, above all in Russia and Japan and India and China, are eye openers for adults, not only as information, which, though genuine and helpful, is the least of their merits or responsibilities, but in the line of getting us to wonder at man and nature. It goes without saying that pictures must be honest and not propaganda.

Studied a bit by the child and then more and more by the youth, the biological world also is a source of

wonder, and should open up to him a vision of ma-
jestic intricacy. We need not preach to him or indoc-
trinate him, but let the facts speak for themselves. The
vision of the bigness of life can be extended, as the
child grows, by an introduction, at least for some
children, to geology, anthropology, ethnology, and
ecology. Really good "wonder books" on all these
and many other subjects are now published; for instance, the Random House "All About" series: all
about mountains, all about snakes, and all about birds,
and so on; and if a little school, tax-supported or not
tax-supported, is too poor to buy a supply of such
books, the State is obliged to make the books available: not for the sake of the church to which the
child does or does not belong, but for the good of
the child and for the common good. Practically speaking, too, we want scientists: well, here is a way to
help to get them—surround children in school, in
every and any school, with such books. Some children love to see what "happens" in chemistry, too, and
to learn how to make things "happen." Few can get
much out of the greatness revealed to us in the study
of physics, and fewer can go far enough to be able
to stand in awe before the harmony and beauty of
the world of mathematics.

We have been speaking of majesty and greatness:
in God, in man, and in nature. Not that we suppose
God and man to belong in no way to nature; each
has "a nature," and is a "natural" something in the

sense of being found by man and not made by man; and the totality of things—God, and man, and sub-human things—found by man and not made by man, add up to what we call "nature," "the world," "reality," or the universe. All of them together are the "given" and are "nature" in the old Greek usage for things not in the first place made by us or subject to our will and our control; the latter things fall in Greek terminology under "art." The Greeks dichotomized everything into "art" and "nature," and the medievals into "art" and "will," and men in modern times into "man" and "nature." Whatever the terms, it would seem a shame if any teacher or school were overcome by timidity and littleness of soul and, wittingly or unwittingly, robbed the child of the chance to see the majesty of nature.

Many ways are available for summing up what we have been saying. We want the child to experience, as he will unless he is terribly orphaned, what William James happily called "the warmth and intimacy of the contemplated me," and also to feel almost the same warmth and intimacy in the life of his home, with his parents and brothers and sisters, that he feels within himself. He comes, in himself and in his home, to an intimate love-knowing. The security, the dependence-independence which we feel in our home, is so close to us that we hardly notice it, let alone notice its value and its simple majesty. It could hardly be taught: it has to be learned. The child needs the sense of belonging, and the sense of the greatness of belonging; he needs the meaning and good of it—a sense, a meaning, a good which we need not explain to him. Here is a world, his world by the way; and, "There's no place like home" are simple enough words to try to express the reality. But then he should have a chance to acquire the sense of belonging and of "at homeness" in other communities: in the neighborhood, in the church, in the nation; and a sense not only of belonging, but of community, and of security, and of greatness.

He needs the same multiple and yet simple sense in relation to the universe itself. The now somewhat common attempt to tear man apart from the universe, to set man completely over against nature, to make man a sort of enemy of God and nature, has been a forced and unnatural position. As C. S. Lewis has said in a remarkable essay: [1] You cannot have it both ways: either the universe means something, or man means nothing: if we have meaning, we do not alone have meaning: you cannot tear man out of the total context and find meaning in him and thus stow him away (said Lewis) in a *faubourg*, and let the rest run on as if a meaningless universe.

Our point here is, that for sensing and "getting" a vision of greatness, the child needs a prior sense of

[1] C. S. Lewis, "The Personal Heresy in Criticism"; *Essays and Studies* (by members of the English Association), v. 19 (1934), pp. 1–28.

meaning and security and "at homeness" under his parents' roof, in the local community with school included, in the church, and in the wide universe. He does not need to be formally taught this, but has a right not to have this good, so natural to mankind, stolen from him. Of course, as Thomas Mann said in *The Magic Mountain*, a man's time has, like it as we will, to teach him either "yes" or "no" or an "empty silence" on the great question, which we have dared to say is back of all great visions: the great question of "meaning" or "no meaning."

Another way to say these things is to say that the child, whatever his age, though differently for different ages, is to see that he himself also is to be great: that he belongs to and is to belong to a great church, a great nation, to do a great work within those societies, and again to be great in creating beauty and seeing beauty and in all the knowings of science, philosophy, and theology. Of course, the mere child would at most dimly sense any of this, and yet one notices that children do seem to feel that it is great to be a member of the Church; the Church herself, in the eyes of parents and teachers and society as a whole, being seen as world-wide, strong, invincible, imperturbable. Truth itself as resplendent, beauty and sanctity as resplendent—the child has a right to catch a glimpse of such greatness. The child has a right to great things and to "the mysterious calm of souls groping for infinite things."

All the same, the child must very early in his education begin to discipline his mind and will and affections. He must learn to bend his mind to the doing of exact sums and to the exact spelling of two- and three-syllable words. With his learning-life disciplined and shaped and cupped to know sapientially and to know prudentially—that is, as a wise man and as a saint—he begins to be prepared to absorb, and we are happy to help him absorb, all human and earthly and heavenly things, things rich enough to fill a new "Benedicite." And we hope that he or some of his fellows will learn to write that modern "Benedicite" and that all will learn to sing it.

>)((

Index

Adelard, 26

Academic societies, participation in, 156-7

Activists and learning, 102-3

Adler, Morimer, on teaching moral virtue, 131

Adult education, Catholic, 164-5

Alcoholism, 135

Alcuin and learning, 1, 25, 161

Alter, Karl, Archbishop, 88-9

American Philosophical Association, 156-7

American pragmatic temper, 120-1

Anselm, St., on Christian philosophy, 59

Apology and learning, 28; *see* End

Apostolate of learning: for Catholic clergy, 167-9; in all fields, 7; "things to do," 143-70

Aristotle: first cause in practical order, 20; how we know, 31-2, 105-6; humility, 42; knowledge, 33; learning moral virtue, 131-6, 140, 143; liberal ends and values, 92; natural desire to

Aristotle (*continued*)
know, 117; Plato's leveling, 81n.; prudence, 128; teaching moral virtue, 131; world meaning, 38-40; *see* Intuition

Arnold, Thomas, vision of greatness, 176-7

Art as learning, 123-5

Ascoli, Max, on social education, 131

Athens and learning, 1, 25

Augustine, St.: Christian philosophy, 59-60; man's greatness, 176; pagan learning, 24-5

Baltimore Councils and Catholic schools, 11-12

Bell, Bernard Iddings, on secularized schools, 83n.

Benedicite, new, 192

Bergson, influence on Dewey, 114

Better, the, defeating the good, 102-3

Blanshard, Paul, lacking freedom, 6, 27-8, 81-2

Blueprint for a Catholic University, 12n., 99n.